BUDDHA

SPIRITUALITY FOR LEADERSHIP & SUCCESS

W0036471

Ultimate Spiritual Lessons,
based on the PowerTalks and MysticTalks of

PRANAY

Published 2025

FiNGERPRINT!
Prakash Books

 Fingerprint Publishing
 @FingerprintP
 @fingerprintpublishingbooks
www.fingerprintpublishing.com

ISBN: 978 93 9039 182 0

Preface

Gautam Buddha is arguably the most influential person ever in the study of human consciousness. He is considered the ninth avatar in the ancient Indian philosophy of divine cyclic manifestation, and the paragon of virtue when it comes to instilling values for life and leadership within human beings. Particularly during the tough times being faced by the world today, Buddha's teachings assume an even greater importance.

Buddha's influence is far-reaching and profound. For example, Japanese management theory is based largely on Buddha's key principles in one way or another. Steve Jobs (a practising Buddhist) built Apple Inc. after being powerfully influenced by Zen aesthetics, which are offshoots of Buddha's most profound teachings (the whole basis of Apple is Zen-like). The beauty of 'Buddha's way' is that literal words are not as important as the cultivation of insight *(prajna)*, a spiritual attitude towards all things, and understanding the underlying principles that determine excellence in all spheres of life. His spiritually inspired wisdom principles and keys touch all aspects of human behaviour, including leadership psychology and the spirit of teamwork, and are particularly relevant for creating values that can lead to higher achievement and real fulfilment.

Leaders throughout history—Ashoka the Great, Oriental emperors, Japan's Samurai warlords, and so on— have been deeply influenced by Buddha's consciousness teachings. The West was influenced in a rather subtle way: Alexander's expedition to India was not just military, but also one of ideas where he carried back several aspects of Buddha's mystic philosophy and integrated them with the West's.

This book highlights key principles of Buddha's root-level consciousness teachings, which have great importance in shaping success, and in shaping leadership virtues that are admired, followed, and most of all— respected!

Pranay

"He who is full of faith and virtue,
In whatever land he travels,
Is respected everywhere!"
Gautam Buddha

Contents

CHAPTER - 1

Monk and Warrior

LESSON: The Buddha's greatest gift to the world is the idea of serene and blissful awareness within ourselves: if that is established, you excel in all things and realize your highest potential. The right attitude is a relaxed yet totally awakened ('bodhi') consciousness. Then, whether you are a monk or a warrior, or indeed a leader of any kind, your work attains great and true success: outwardly dynamic, inwardly undisturbed, and full of peaceful fulfilment. This becomes especially important for individuals and leaders facing big challenges or crisis situations, such as those of current times: pandemics, economic unpredictability, environmental disasters, societal or interpersonal conflict.

> "Bliss is attainable by everyone
> who walks on the noble path."
> Gautam Buddha

Gautam Buddha's path is for both the monk and the warrior. In other words, his spiritual teachings have profound lessons for us on two dimensions: the mystical as well as the material. No matter where we are, in what position or field of work, the core lessons of Buddhism hold true and can lead to far greater excellence. It could be in business, politics, sports, arts, or any other field: the fundamentals of success and good leadership remain the same. Dignity, respect, calmness, brilliant clarity, intuitive leadership—these are all traits and hallmarks which can hold us in good stead as leaders in any sphere. Which is why Buddha's message was not only emulated by spiritual aspirants but by those who followed the 'warrior's code': for example, Buddhism inspired martial artists in China, samurai warriors following the 'Bushido' code in Japan, and Japanese business leaders for their work culture and business ethics.

Dignity in leadership and respect for the leader within the team, amongst all the members, is one of the vital lessons to extrapolate from Gautam Buddha's principles. It creates a sober yet massively powerful work ethic.

The ancient Buddhists were very fond of using the

Pali word *ariya* (*arya* in Sanskrit). It means noble-hearted and noble-minded. It implies somebody who carries a calm sense of dignity, self-respect, and respect for others. In the Buddha's vision this is a quality not only of the monk, but of every other human being who aspires for strength and excellence in life. Be that person a warrior, a king, a leader, a businessman, or of any other profession.

It is an underlying principle. Without self-respect and self-dignity, respect for others, respect for values, everything is meaningless. The way of the Buddhist monk is all about cultivating this sense of deep dignity for life, respect for life. And this is a quality we can all imbibe. Because having these qualities and being conscious of these qualities, we become more natural and spontaneous in action. We become far more dynamic and filled with energy because now we experience a feeling of oneness with the universe, a feeling of being more powerfully rooted in life in a noble, spiritually courageous manner.

In that way you grow, you send out your highest energies into the world. You are recognized for your own intrinsic potential. You bring the best and highest energies to what you do, with dignity and respect. There cannot be true success or great leadership without these values, nor good co-operative and heartfelt teamwork.

This insight and principle applies to teams, particularly. The first essence of a good team is this: there must be respect for each other in the team. That is why in sports you would often notice that sometimes, even when a particular team has some very strong *individual* players, when they come together to play, they don't necessarily win. In fact, they may lose to a side which might otherwise not comprise of so many gifted players! The key differentiator often is the degree of mutual respect within the team. Sometimes the 'weaker' team displays this 'spirit' of respectful teamwork far better, hence making the team far more effective! Within the team whose players have more of a respect for each other, a quiet dignity and power is created. That is the noble path: it leads to more joyful enthusiasm and energy within. And that leads to great leadership and team results. Through such mutual dignity comes true victory: this learning is at the heart of Buddha's way for both the monk and the warrior! It is a core, subtle principle that the samurai unit may for example demonstrate, and is a key part of Buddhism-inspired Japanese work ethics too. This ethic is at the heart of two of the greatest institutions in human history: the Budhha-inspired Nalanda and Vikramashila universities of the ancient world.

Going back again to the analogy of sports teams will be useful: it captures the heart of the message. You will find these principles apply well for captains or leaders of sports teams. Some captains might not be the greatest individual players, but they manifest such good leadership qualities that they are able to lift the team. There's some x-factor in them which is able to make people shine forth through their inspiration. This often arises from the sense of dignity and self-belief they give to individuals within the team; the sense of respect, the eye for detail that they have for others. And the time they spend motivating others, bringing out their self-belief with great energy.

So, for teamwork this is very essential. It is a fundamental value, and it is all about knowing your own power from within. It could be as an individual, or it could be as the team. What dignity does and what respect does is that it takes away the fear of each other, or the suspicion of each other. Teams often fail because of subtle suspicions within the team: people are scared of each other in some manner, or wary of each other. And this implies a weakness of values, the primary value being mutual respect.

It is not about being 'slapped on one cheek and turning the other cheek' (which is perhaps more of a 'moral' attitude)! Rather, it is about a mutual recognition of each other's human values and attributes. And so doing, the bonds are strengthened because they are based on faith in one another, belief in one another. And where there is faith and belief in the team, there is bound to be great success!

Hence, while building the team, the leader has to understand very clearly that it is not about just joining the different skills of each other. It is about recognizing the purpose of the team in entirety, and the spiritual purpose of any team is essentially to uplift each other's energy to its maximum creativity. If that happens, the team will spontaneously move towards success in its aims. The sum of the parts should add up to more than just the individual attributes.

What mutual dignity and mutual respect do is that they take away doubt from one another, creating an atmosphere charged with a positive vibe. That is the kind of energy every team must have. While doubt is a good tool sometimes, it is belief and deep faith in one's team which is required, because eventually that is the most inspirational factor for a human gathering. When people come together, they want a recognition of who they are. Not in an egoistic or self-important way, but just a human recognition of what they stand for. If the leader can give them that, then he or she is successful. Quiet dignity within a team creates a great blissful energy and power within it.

The Buddha's monastic order or *sangha* was a very good example of teamwork, and of these values. It in fact marks a turning point for religion itself, a template for what it means to demonstrate dignity as a group or unit, and live nobly together, lifting up the entirety of each others' energies in a manner that best met the leader's (Buddha) objectives. For the first time in human civilization, such a large mass of people from all backgrounds came together and existed together nobly for a common spiritual cause. The sangha comprised different kinds of people, from various backgrounds: some came from aristocratic backgrounds, some from poor backgrounds, some from royal backgrounds, some from super rich backgrounds, some from the warrior class, and so on. But how Buddha shaped the monastic order as a leader is remarkable. It was about recognizing the individuality of each member in the monastic order. For Ananda his attendant for example, he had his own way. For the other people he had another way. So his approach was always centred around recognition of people's individual strengths. This is a key insight for leaders to pay conscious attention to.

Ultimately there is no substitute for personal recognition of people in a team. The example of Buddha's sangha is a metaphor: it can be used to understand team dynamics in any situation. In a business unit, for example, comprising senior CXOs, there has to be a mutual respect, there has to be a dignity between them. They might get into arguments, but there's some basic respect which must exist at the heart of the team. If that gets strengthened, the team gets strengthened. It's essentially all about strengthening the roots of the team or the organization.

In politics, the problem is often lack of dignity and mutual respect, of deep suspicions of one another, and of people in general. This leads to nasty and negative politics. It creates a great cancer in society. Politics often becomes something where the participants are just pulling each other down like crabs in a basket. But true teamwork means pushing each other up, and that is the essential message of the Buddha.

The word 'Bodhisattva' is very important in this context. It implies one who is seeking liberation not only for herself or himself, but also for others. The Bodhisattva carries on making endeavours for others to flourish and find self-enlightenment. And the Buddha himself is said to be standing at the gate of Nirvana, refusing to enter till every being in the universe attains enlightenment! Now this is the example of an ultimate leader. A person who is willing to do anything for the entirety of the team (or in this case, his universal family). But it is metaphorical. The whole meaning is that the great leader is one who is willing to take such a stand of dignity and nobleness, that he never deserts his team when it comes to support and values. She or he stands by it with mutual respect, and so doing, strengthens its roots. People start regarding such a leader more and more. People start understanding such a leader's vision more and more. And thereby, the leader's leadership position starts becoming deeper and more powerful. But this power is not for harming anybody: it is the power of helping the entirety of the team effort.

Every individual should absorb this lesson. Just as the monk and the warrior both should have dignity, self-respect, mutual respect, so should all leaders. Through that would come faith and belief in one another within the team. Ultimately all these spiritually inspired values, at the very soul of Buddha's message, add up to a powerfully dynamic and forceful team, which the leader can take to great heights of excellence.

CHAPTER-2

Action Born of Inner Coolness Has Great Power

LESSON: Observing your own consciousness, become absolutely cool and composed within.

One of the biggest contributions of the Buddha to the world, and to human consciousness, is the understanding that all action which is born out of coolness or out of the meditative state has great power. This is extremely important to understand from the success and leadership perspectives. Actions which are born out of a silence of being, a coolness of being *(sitibhaava/sheetalta)*, are infinitely more powerful than actions which are born out of the noise of the mind, of anxiety, confusion, and so on. It is basically about coming to a meditative state, and then acting. All great success and leadership attributes—inspiration, courage, commitment, purpose, determination/resolve, clarity of vision, integrity, trustworthiness, power of expression, accountability, right decision-making, correct timing, effective delegation, and empathetic empowerment— flow from the unlimited power of inner coolness in one way or another.

The greatest human beings ever born have had this capacity, to function out of a state of inner coolness. Even in the midst of their intensity, there has been something within them which has been almost meditative, absorbed, and cool. Hence, whatever they manifested in the world of action has had great beauty and creativity. It basically has to do with deep behavioural patterns.

The key technique Gautam Buddha taught to attain inner coolness is *Anapanasati*—watching one's breath. This act of breath-watching is key to Vipassana or awareness-cultivation, and can be extended to all activities: in any situation, bring your attention back to your breath. Then, even in the midst of difficult situations, you can instantly come back to your inner self and its spiritually cool, tranquil quality. Watching the breath is a practical manner of creating an inner state of calm. This technique has also been described by Lord Shiva to Parvati. The teaching of inner coolness is not about any particular technique, though; it is about being firm in the resolve, 'No matter what the outer situation, no matter what the circumstances, in my inner world I will be calm this moment. I will be inwardly still, relaxed, cool!' This very resolve is relevant to leaders especially, as leadership requires acting with inner calmness and poise. One can in fact choose *not* to follow any technique at all: this very resolve creates an inner vibe of cool calm. Simply remember to refer back to your inward serenity instead of identifying with outer events. It is the idea of moving away from superficial thoughts that crowd upon us at every moment, and tapping instead our inner layers of being that are deeper and are more fundamental to our spiritual reality.

The crux of the idea is this: in order to be effective, transcend the screen of the mind and allow the greater energy which resides deep within you to act within the world. That creative energy can only be tapped into when you are very cool in heart and mind. Action generated through this inward coolness is imbued with the courage, power, and grace of something which is special. Now, you must have come across people in your workplace who are constantly jumping about 'beating their own drum', making a noise about their vision and so on, but when it comes to action they are found wanting. This is a highly irritating trait often found in leaders. Yes, sometimes to get the task done you have to have the right kind of publicity, you have to create a certain noise, you have to marshal the troops whom you are leading in order to win the battle. But the most inspiring quality in a human being is the ability to have great courage combined with coolness. This brings about a radical consciousness in the way we perceive things, process them mentally and emotionally, and ultimately act!

So we have to understand that it is the combination of courage and coolness which is the hallmark of a great leader. You can see it in some great leaders like Subhash Chandra Bose, the great thinker-warrior who unified Indians at a very deep psycho-spiritual level. He was greatly energetic, full of action in the midst of struggle and battle. Yet there was something deeply calm, cool, and collected about him. It is almost like he was functioning out of a meditative trance. The same principle at work can be found in all truly great leaders.

Buddha was constantly inspiring people to create a coolness of being within themselves. This mystic philosophy was eventually transported to China and Japan. In China it manifested as the Shaolin martial arts: the martial artist, even in the midst of his martial arts, is to be extremely cool and collected. Then does the power of the empty fist—'kung fu'—and so on have any real meaning. In fact, in the modern age Bruce Lee signified this very effectively. He used to talk about it very philosophically: about how a person is to be like water flowing into any vessel and taking its shape. River water is cool and flowing, yet has great power. So 'being like water' is an essential Buddha-quality which martial artists and people in every field were supposed to master. That is the whole basis of Zen philosophy. The samurai were supposed to be really cool in their method of functioning. Even the ninja, in their martial code, were supposed to be extremely cool and collected! It is an underlying principle of Buddhism.

The most dynamic people you will find are those who can have courage under fire. But even under fire they remain cool and collected. So too the greatest soldiers in any battle. You will see the greatest generals have this ability. On the sports field, you will have seen the greatest sportsmen have this ability. Look at the difference between two Indian cricket players, Sachin Tendulkar and Vinod Kambli: they were almost equal in skill. In fact, a lot of people said in the earlier days Kambli had some great and special talent. But the difference between them was perhaps the question of coolness of character. Sachin Tendulkar manifests it beautifully: always calm, cool, collected, yet always courageous. Hence, he emerged as a great dynamic sportsman who is not only loved but is deeply respected by people. So he has a true 'thought leadership' role as a sportsperson.

He has become an icon, a charismatic example of a fine sportsman.

This principle for leadership applies in all fields. You can see it in the world of business, you can see it in the world of politics, in the world of religion, and so on. Those who can be really cool and collected under fire are the ones to be remembered as the greatest leaders. You can find this principle in Nelson Mandela, even when vilified by the apartheid South African government. You'll never find Mandela with a facial visage which is not cool, calm, and collected. He's always got an appearance of coolness in him. Hence his level of respect as a leader in the twentieth century is almost unmatched. In fact, he made his opponents look stupid because they were reacting out of hatred, out of anger. All that Mandela acted out of was courage coupled with coolness. So this is a very essential leadership quality, and Buddha is a core source of such teachings.

Look at the Aikido martial art of Japan, or the Judo martial art (again, both inspired by Buddha's broader principles for excellence in all spheres of life). The martial artist uses the other person's energy very coolly to overthrow them, to defeat them. And that is what a good leader does. You can only do that with the sense of coolness. If you are attacked by the opponent, you simply utilize his own energy, and effortlessly combine it with your own. Then you will become victorious.

So it is a question of spontaneity; allowing the spontaneous coolness of your mind to spill over into your action. That creates immense dynamism.

The miracle of the Buddha is that he never believed in showing miracles on the material plane. He used to say that the only real miracle resides in our own consciousness. To tap into these miracles requires a mind which is silent, which can go deep, which can go to the very source of ourselves. And in that source is an immense coolness. At the level of soul, at the level of our innate being, there is absolute coolness. It is like the ocean: on the surface, the waves of the ocean are very boisterous and noisy. But the deeper we go into the ocean, the quieter the flow. So, depth requires dynamism. Depth requires coolness. Similarly, you will find this principle if you look at a photograph of deep space taken by the Hubble Deep Field telescope. You will find that in the cosmos itself there is an almost unbelievable level of action, there is immense dynamism, there is massive energy of stars being formed, galaxies rotating and so on. But when you look at the larger image in totality, it will give you a sense of coolness. At the heart of creation itself this quality of sublime tranquillity exists, even though it may seem that there is great flux and disorder at the material level.

Hence, look at the vaster picture of things with a sense of coolness. Just as the eagle surveys all from a great height! Have an eagle's eye view of things, and then you will become more aware, more conscious, more insightful into things as a leader. The eagle flies very high in the sky, where it is established in a space of coolness. It has a view which is unmatched. It is able to look at things very coolly from that great height. The cool and collected eye of the eagle is the kind of vision which every person must seek to cultivate. It is the master key for success and leadership, inspired by Buddha's insights into reality.

CHAPTER-3

Position Can Be Lost, but Not Inner Power

LESSON: The Buddha stands for infinite self-power. Nothing can alter the power of that which is within you. It is unlimited. Being established in this understanding, a good leader is never shaken by any untoward circumstance or crisis.

Why is the spiritual way so important when it comes to leadership and success? It is essentially because through it we can come to an understanding that we have an inner power *(antara bala)*, and this inner power cannot be destroyed. Even if an outer circumstance is detrimental to us, even if we lose a position, the individuality of our inner power is to be so bright that we can overcome all odds. And that is the whole purpose of Buddha's teaching: to make us inwardly enlightened to a degree where all outer questions are taken care of on their own.

Life is a very unpredictable process. It is like the mind: the mind keeps changing thought images, changing feelings. So too is life; it keeps changing. Yet beyond the material circumstances of the world and beyond the thoughts of the mind there lies an inner power which is yours. Do not get confined to only matter. Mysticism is going beyond the confinement of material understanding and into the understanding of the original sources of life itself. Understand your life energy *(satti),* and make it powerful.

Buddha's effort is to strengthen your life energy. Strengthening of life energy means strengthening of your inner power. You are touching the centre of yourself, and in so doing you become not only powerful, but you also become relaxed. You also become peaceful. You become aware that you just have to remember who you are within you! Remind yourself that you are beyond body, beyond mind, beyond circumstances. And then you become stronger and stronger. So in this way the monk and the warrior both understand that their inner power cannot be destroyed, come what may.

When a person is grounded in this understanding, automatically his or her actions become imbued with great force of spirit and mind. A person of understanding has a directness of clarity. You can see it and feel it in his vibe. His life becomes a celebration of consciousness. And people become attracted to such a person. It is a natural process.

A human being seems very small, but within us we contain infinities upon infinities of life energy and inner power. That is the whole teaching of the Buddha. That is what he came to represent. And added to that is his view that we are to share this inner power with people through whatever work we undertake creatively, with a feeling of inner radiance. If we can do that, something gets communicated to others. We become emptied of our anxiety and filled with a self-confidence. And leadership is all about having self-confidence.

The Buddha's vision was very novel and transformative because though he did not affirm the existence of a 'god', he says each one of us has a god-like energy of intuitive perception and consciousness, of inner value. So bring this god-like ability into your understanding. Then everything becomes a victory in life, because you have become deeply courageous with the feeling that nothing can defeat you in the inner domain. Motivation and inspiration are all about these kind of feelings. If a person feels like this and pulsates with this feeling, he is also able to transfer it onto his team. And if you can transfer this onto your team, you become a great motivating force in their lives. Essentially, leadership is about becoming a motivating force in the team's existence. Make the team also believe that it is their inner power which is important. When their sense of working together is combined with all their inner power as a unified whole, then results have to come. And they come in a manner which is innovative, creative. If you place the 'result' before the 'group energy', you are making a mistake. The group energy is very important. It is the key element for higher achievement, fulfilment, real collaborative and shared success.

You can observe that within every team or group there exists a particular vibe, a particular energy. Some teams simply pulsate with positive energy, and some teams are almost dead in vital energy—devoid of the spiritual and emotional quality of passion. And those teams which are devoid of the quality of passion are hardly creative. What is creativity in a team? It simply implies that people are willing to grow, that people are willing to exist in a manner where they are ready to take quantum jumps into the next level of innovativeness. Nothing scares them. So it's key to take away fear from the team consciousness, and the way a leader can do it is by reminding them of their inner power. Harness this power, gather this energy, channelize it towards your aim. Essentially, that is what good leadership means. So the leader has to be alert to these virtues, and enhance these. Take away the negatives, and the positive remains. There has to be a feeling of spontaneity and joy in a team. Through that only can the team become an instrument of great achievement. Otherwise the team remains ordinary.

In mankind's coming years, the question of team energy will become more and more important. As far as skill-based work goes, a lot of that will be handed over to artificial intelligence. But as far as human life energy goes, that is something still within the domain of human consciousness. So, teams which are able to create positivity in team energy will become formidable. And that is where we need to imbibe learnings from the Buddha to understand what it means to create a sensibility of inner power, a sensibility of higher energy, a sensibility of greater intuitive and almost mystical creativity. The inner feeling has to enter into outer action. If you can facilitate that in the team in a positive manner, you become successful as an all-round leader. Else not.

It is never about intellectual capacity alone. Human beings do not work through pure intellect. Human beings work more through feelings, through impulses. Buddha went deep into this: behind thoughts are feelings, and beyond feelings is the underlying, procreative consciousness. So, imbue the team with feelings of power at that root consciousness level. That must flow from your own intuitive sense, constantly inspiring people. From the vibe of deep inspiration alone comes the success of value-creation, with reference to real and actual material things too. Create it as an authentic energy, and then the team will not fail you. Because then at the centre of the team's innermost being would come about a purity of power.

Buddha used to say that it is not eventually the quantum of time that is important, as far as realizing your Buddhahood or enlightenment *(sambodhi)* goes. You can become enlightened even in a few seconds if you put your heart and mind to it, if you put your total power into it, if you invest your energy into it! That is the miracle of spiritually inspired principles. And so, we must learn also how to apply these principles to create our own little miracles as leaders, whatever our position or work is. It is simply a question of attitude: of how we feel within, how we emphasize our own inner power, and how in turn we are able to imbue and inspire our teams with a sense of inner power. That is the real challenge for a leader. It just requires us to become more aware of it, in order to bring it into practical action.

Wisdom Is Transcendental to the Mind

LESSON: The cultivation of intuitive wisdom, where emotions and thoughts are calm and the higher virtues of empathy and right-mindfulness are awakened, is the duty of every responsible leader.

From the Buddhist perspective, real wisdom (prajna) is always transcendental to the mind. Real wisdom includes empathy *(metta)* and love *(sneha),* both. Without empathy or the ability to appreciate and understand others, and without love (love for work, love for people, love for one's own being) wisdom does not dawn. Now, this is very important from the leadership perspective. Because eventually a leader should *lead through wisdom.* That is the most important thing.

A leader without such wisdom is likely to lead people into hellish situations. So, genuine wisdom is a very essential part of one's leadership role. It does not mean the wisdom of a Buddha, but it means the wisdom of that which is transcendental to what people ordinarily think. Then only do you have value as a leader. If you're simply doing what others think, then you shouldn't be a leader. A leader has that extra x-factor, and that should be wisdom.

As the world faces more crises of every kind, wisdom is needed even more in leadership. This is very significant to understand. In the Buddhist perspective it is called applied mindfulness *(satipatthaana)*. It is not at all about becoming a meditator or becoming a renunciate, an ascetic. It is rather about bringing the quality of mindfulness into your being, and through this quality of mindfulness, wisdom spontaneously dawns. Otherwise, we are simply dictated by our repetitive thoughts. You can look at a lot of world leaders: they themselves seem so confused, how will they lead vast numbers of people to well-being? And that has been the trend throughout history. Without wisdom, leaders have led nations only into conflict, into war, into bloodshed. But this principle applies to any endeavour in human life. It could be business, it could be a commercial objective, or of any other sort.

There must be an intuitive part in every sort of leadership—business, political, organizational, scientific, technological, artistic, etc.—which is transcendental to ordinary thinking. And what is this intuitive part? This intuitive part is only activated by a feeling of well-being and love in those who lead into the world. Bringing love into that which you do connects people to you. Eventually, this has business dividends also, because it is based on something solid and true.

There are some values which are the innermost core pillars for success. There is no substitute for them. One of those values is working through wisdom, and leading through wisdom. Let the intelligence of the cosmos function through you. That is the ultimate aim. Leaders often think, 'I am somebody!', and through this very thinking they get trapped in ego. Through the ego, they have only a small window into the vastness of their potential.

There is no substitute for wisdom in the world: cunning or cleverness can never replace wisdom, because essentially cunning does not bring bliss. Cunning does not bring innovative breakthroughs. Cunning does not bring transformation. What brings transformation is acting through mindfulness! Through mindfulness comes wisdom. There are a lot of speakers or clever talkers, leaders who are very convincing at the level of feelings or thought. But eventually what they do is they pull people downwards, because instead of acting out of wisdom they act out of ego. It's that simple.

Wisdom is about knowing the inner truth of things. It is about knowing the inner truth of people. It is about knowing the inner truth of how best to serve. That is what dynamic leadership truly means. And this is a secret of consciousness. You see, when a person has a consciousness of empathy, he creates a vibe of empathy around him. All that he does has a touch of this empathy. Hence, all his actions create a cycle of empathy, and where there is empathy there is general well-being. Because the right things are done at the right time, with the right intention. The intentions are correct, and where the intentions are correct, the results—whatever they may be—cannot be entirely wrong. Out of noble intention are born noble deeds. Noble deeds cannot be born out of egoistic interest. And the great leader is somebody who keeps doing noble deeds, whatever his capacity. He might not be in a very important position, he might not be leading many people, but whatever is in his capacity he does with empathy. He does not misuse his leader's space. Instead there is a deep longing within a leader to make people's potentiality sprout. And he does whatever is in his power to make that possible.

In Buddhist terminology the dawning of wisdom is called the blooming of the 'lotus' within one's being. The lotus flower is taken as a symbol of great purity and wisdom. Because it has the ability to live amidst murky water but at the same time it has the wisdom to survive, flourish, flower, be beautiful, be at its utmost grandeur and potential. And that is the way the leader should be. So, the Buddhist symbol of the lotus becomes very important: it is a reminder of the transcendental nature of wisdom. Transcend the circumstances you are in. Transcend the limitations you are placed under. And bloom forth to your best! Then people will automatically notice you. You will automatically move upward. There is no need to be anything else but yourself. Let the spiritual lotus in your heart blossom not only within yourself, but within your work. Yes, it does require willpower and resolve. It requires a great resolution of heart and mind. But it in fact requires more than willpower: it requires enough courage in the heart to function out of that which is wise and which is beneficial.

Again, the good leader is one who uses his own ability and his own potential to take a great leap beyond what people are ordinarily thinking. And the only way to surpass the ordinary is to become liberated from your own conditioning, your own confining ideas. Let the mind open up. Liberate yourselves from your past, your thoughts, from the trap of what you have known previously. That is the only way to move towards an innovative leadership space. It is also very mystically and spiritually liberating, but at a practical level what it does is, it gives you a capacity for inventiveness. Because you don't feel occupied and full by the yesterday that you *had*. You once again are available to whatever circumstance is confronting you, and this is what true transcendence means: to move into newer spaces, better spaces of consciousness. It requires a certain patience and silence within the heart, and that is also the hallmark of a good Buddhist monk.

Things which Buddha used to talk extensively about are silence and patience as the route to real wisdom. Both these virtues enable you to become rooted in wisdom, enable you to become transcendental to the mind. So utilize your private moments to be more silent, to be more mindful. And then you will find a great energy integrating within yourself, becoming freely available to you, to utilize like a dynamo when you need it in your leadership role.

CHAPTER-5

Be Light

LESSON: Becoming conscious of the spiritual reality that you are ultimately beyond your mind's anxious thoughts and worries, makes you feel light and intensely dynamic as a leader!

The quality of dynamism is the quality of being light, of not being overly 'weighed down' or worried about yourself. And great leaders have this ability. At critical moments, they are able to work in a manner where they are not worried about themselves. Wisdom lies in knowing that we are a part of the wholeness of creation, and that this wholeness will take care of things. There has to be a liberated quality within the leader, if she or he is to be dynamic. You cannot carry the burden of self-worry or self-anxiety, and still expect to be dynamic. Buddha's way was to make people unburden themselves of foolish notions of anxiety *(ashanka)* and worry. Rather, he used to encourage them to look at the greater picture. The unburdening of thought and anxiety impulses is a key fundamental of Tibetan Mahamudra Buddhism, as taught by Naropa and others.

Often, when people used to come to Buddha to become disciples, he used to send them to the cemetery, where dead bodies are burnt. The whole idea is conveying to them that 'eventually you too have to die, so what are you worried about?!' So, those who wanted to be part of the *sangha* or monastic order of Buddha experienced and internalized this fact deeply: that eventually death is going to come to us any moment, so why be worried? And once that fear goes, you become dynamic! That is the whole secret of dynamism. Then, you are ready to meet any circumstance with the joyfulness of energy which you have within you. Otherwise, people are constantly low in life energy, somewhat anxious or afraid of future outcomes. But the way of the leader, the way of the warrior, the way of the truly accomplished achiever is to move along with the current of life as swiftly as possible. And not with any burden in mind. If the mental burden is there, you cannot really move fast and swift. The good and dynamic leader sheds mental burdens within his own style of thought and action, and helps those he leads do so too.

Essentially, it is all about understanding that you are to create this inward transformation, this inward understanding of liberating yourself. And then you have nothing to fear! The earnest understanding within will take care of the outer. The opposite of this situation is leaders who are so obsessed by their own worries, that they are not able to lead efficiently. And you'll find that this is one of the most important psycho-spiritual differences between people who are dynamic and those who are not.

People are often fearful that something will happen to them: they're worried about their chair, their position, their health, their wealth, and so on. So doing, they cannot really be liberated and dynamic leaders. They might be achievers in their own way, but to be a great leader requires an extra quality. It requires a realization that one's inevitable fate is only death, so let's try and maximize our dynamism while we can, without worry! And it also requires a realization that the wholeness of creation is more powerful than us: it takes care of things as it needs. All that we can do is act dynamically.

Hence, don't cling to your problems, don't cling to your doubts. Let go of them. And then the possibility of becoming swift and efficient in action as a leader truly dawns. Throw away the burdens which have been created in your own mind. That is the most essential act in order to become a tremendous force of charisma. Then only can you transcend your self-limitations, and move into a situation where you act so freely, with such confidence and energy, that other people are immediately responsive to your vibe.

People are always responsive to a vibe of true confidence. And the way to move towards true confidence is to liberate yourself at your innermost source of being. A leader must inspire others to believe in themselves to do so.

True self-belief and self-confidence imply playfulness and creative energy. These qualities help us transcend the ordinary and move into the extraordinary spaces of life. Make your inner problems disappear, then outer problems can be taken care of. People have become so stuck with their inner problems—emotional, psychological, and so on—that they don't have energy to solve outer problems. And a leader is essentially one who has to solve outer problems. But firstly, at an inward level he has to solve his problems.

Buddha is concerned about your inner. Because the first thing is that inner domain: everything begins from there. If that is clear, all becomes clear. If that is murky and unclear, all becomes murky and unclear. Feel reassured within your being that most of the problems you think about are unreal, imaginary. Create real happiness in yourself, not dependent on other peoples' views, but self-evident. Feel so rich *within* that your outer life acquires the quality of this inward freedom or liberation. That is the first step towards ultimate spiritual liberation *(nibanna/ nirvana)*.

In the subtle psycho-spiritual aspect of life or the mystical aspect of life, it is important how you listen to yourself, respond to yourself, and look at yourself. This is what matters. Because through that you create a similar vibe in reality, in the 'outer' or 'real' world. You throb with that which you believe about yourself. If you are worried about yourself constantly, that is the vibe you throw out into the world. And nobody wants to follow a person whose vibe is one of constant worry! Rather throb with positive energy by getting rid of your psychological problems. And then do you find others respond to this vibe of your energy, because people are automatically attracted to that kind of vibe. Get rid of the conflicts within you, and then do you reach the heart of yourself, then is the energy available for you to achieve higher things as a leader.

Buddha's teachings bring us into an inner tuning and rhythm with our own selves, like an instrument. All we need to do is put ourselves into 'tune' or inner harmony, and when the instrument is in tune then the music that comes out of it is beautiful. If in the first place the instrument has not been tuned, the music cannot be good. We can call the greatest player also, but he will not be able to produce great music out of it. That is the way of human beings at every level: spiritual, psychological, mystical, emotional. And this spills over into our relationships, our work, our businesses or professions. It is a basic principle: tune yourself. And tuning yourself means just putting yourself in a good inner state. Then whatever music comes out of your being as a doer of actions, or as a leader of people, becomes imbued with a different energy. And obviously, when the music that the instrumentalist is producing is beautiful, he will gather listeners. In other words, the leader with inward harmony is more deeply listened to by his or her team. We will simply make more sense; we will become intense. Therefore, let what is past vanish: just concentrate on tuning your instrument at this moment. And then a beautiful future will happen out of this. This principle of inner harmony is a very foundational teaching for leadership.

The problem with a lot of 'positive thinkers' and proponents of 'positive psychology', is that they concentrate on fixing the personality of a person: to make the 'personality' more positive. But they often don't go deeper than that. It is not about personality; it is about going deep into your subconscious levels, and from that point, unburdening yourself of your anxieties! Once you are unburdened, then whatever happens is positive. You don't have to create a mask of positivity. A lot of leaders carry a mask of positivity, but that is not true and authentic leadership. There is no need to play-act. You just need to get into your own essential character, and then the play will unfold on its own.

Life is like a flowing river. If there are no barriers to the river's progress, it will flow on its own: smoothly, dynamically, and powerfully. But if there are barriers, then it gets disturbed. The flow gets disturbed. And in human consciousness, the only barriers are those which we create. Unburden yourself of them. Feel light, and then you become more and more dynamic.

CHAPTER 6

Balance Speed at Work with Festivity

LESSON: Pause and have joyful gratitude for all things, even amidst the most hectic activity. This adds composure, depth, maturity, charisma, and luminosity to all you do as a leader. It places the wonder of life, and your role within its procession of endlessly festive possibilities, in true perspective.

One of the biggest challenges that leaders of today face is to deliver results with great speed. Speed is the essence of this century. Everything needs to happen really, really fast. However, sometimes it is not just getting to the destination as soon as possible which is important, but also the quality of *how* you have made the journey. Otherwise life goes by in a jiffy, and we miss all that we could have taken from life. This is one of the crucial underpinnings of Buddhism, a lesson to learn about the Buddhist way of life. Buddha used to emphasize the 'right way' to walking the path, and then the destination will be reached on its own, both without delay and with a suitable enlightened consciousness. From this teaching came the Zen understanding of 'easiness': implying a consciously slow yet consistent pace in all things. For the question of leadership, this becomes a very important teaching. It is also a vital part of Tibetan Mahamudra Buddhism.

It is very interesting that after the Buddha attained enlightenment, it is said that the gods showered flowers from the heavens. They celebrated his life, his enlightenment, with festivity. All achievements, whether spiritual or material, should be filled with the shower of festive spirit, not just at the end of the journey but during it. The pathways of life itself are to be filled with an inner feeling of festivity. Where we can celebrate every step forward on the road towards our own fulfilment. A very interesting aspect of the Buddha especially in the Orient, is of course the 'Laughing Buddha'. Now, this Laughing Buddha is a very strong example of what it means to find true celebration in life, to celebrate the festival of life with joy and laughter in your heart. It is based on this story of a Buddhist monk whose only renunciation in life or only practice in life was to distribute sweets to poor children!

It is a Japanese story based on a real person called Budai (a manifestation of the Buddha of friendship, the coming Maitreya Buddha). This aspect of Buddhahood is very interesting because it shows you the vastness of Buddhist teaching. Essentially saying that it is the festivity, love, and joy that you're distributing along the way which makes you a true leader! This 'Laughing Buddha', by any conventional standards, may not be taken very seriously but he is bringing to humanity a very essential thing: he's bringing the forgotten joy of life to humanity. And that is what a true leader in the final analysis has to do—bring to you the forgotten joy of living itself, of creativity, of innovativeness, on whatever path it is you have chosen. And the miracle is that the Laughing Buddha becomes a leader in his own right: the children follow him not just for the sweets, but out of sheer joy and ecstasy. It is a deep Buddhistic metaphor for living and leading successfully; about how to become a conveyor and purveyor of festivity, dynamism, bliss, and joy! And in the final analysis, a great leader is one who can create bliss for others.

You must understand that Buddha's path was one of total intensity. He wanted to achieve enlightenment with great speed. But along with that, you would notice a quality of patience. Buddha is a unique combination of both speed and patience. He held nothing back. Speed implies totality, getting results as swiftly as possible. But with the Buddha it also implied waiting with patience, making the journey with patience. And when you make the journey with patience, then you have the ability to create a real relationship with life, and understand the festival of creativity that is this whole cosmic creation. Now, the whole point from the leadership aspect is to enjoy the journey as much as you do getting to the destination. In the end, no destination can be the final destination. The ultimate and final destination is only death. Therefore, it is very important for leaders to not get blinded by their search for results, but also along the way to create as much festivity for their own soul and for others. This eventually marks them out as being of real humanistic value.

History has seen millions of people who have made their mark in some way or the other. But there are some special ones who stand out, who gave humanity a hope that the very process of living can be utterly fulfilling and rewarding. It is not eventually how many dollars in the bank you have, but it is how dignified a life you have led. That is true leadership. Leave that as your leadership legacy. Learn from the Buddha: his every act—his way of walking, his way of talking, his way of communicating with people—was imbued with such a beautiful energy that people were automatically influenced by him. He didn't need to do anything extra. He just did his own thing. And in doing your own thing an immense charisma accrues to you. People start feeling like you are capable of creating a paradise in your own way. In fact, it is said in esoteric Buddhist texts that each human being is a 'creator': we can create our paradise whilst living. So be such a creative leader, who is creating a paradise and revelling in this festival of life at every moment. Then is the quality of life enhanced. This is not antithetical to acquiring results: the new paradigm for leadership has to be one which creates well-being in the leader, and also in those who follow the leader.

Every individual is a potential leader. Gone are the days when leadership simply meant cracking the whip or giving a great speech without really meaning it. Now it is about being able to pull people up from where they are. It is about upliftment, correction, radical positive change, and so on. It is about making people truly believe in a better life, in a better existence for everybody. It is not simply an accumulation of power or money which is important. In fact, if you think of a good futuristic society you will be able to see very clearly that it is things such as joy, camaraderie, cheerfulness, and the ability to get along with others which are more important than anything else. That way, the ecosystem we exist within will also be revived. There has to be a reverence for life, a reverence for fellow beings. Through that comes real mutual respect, holistic and organic development.

One of the main questions of this century has to be this: how do we address all the wrongs of humanity? We are moving towards so many catastrophes and crisis situations, simply because our consumerism has overburdened the earth, destroyed the environment. The next paradigm of leadership has to be one which is much more responsible and alert to things which can create a crisis, be it the environment, be it more and more 'weaponization', be it flora and fauna preservation challenges, and so on. Of course, issues such as human health, education parameters and such also come in, but the essential quality required is a reverence for life. And not just moving with great speed. Celebrate life, celebrate the festival of life. But the celebration does not have to be an orgy of consumerism, an orgy of exploitation. Be a leader who is a true citizen of the world, who is rooted in making his own ecosystem as rich as possible. And eventually the test of a positive leader is one who has made his society, his broader ecosystem as inwardly rich as possible, as joyful and organically unified as possible. That is the ultimate test of a leader. It is a benchmark, and is the ultimate value which a leader can bring.

So, to allow your energy to explode to its best, remember that every step of your journey has to be taken with a sense of positivity, where the most positive presence of yourself leaves an impact upon those who believe in you. And you will find thereby that more and more people start believing in you. Strangely enough, in the film *Forrest Gump*, an apt corollary can be found. Forrest just keeps running. He just does what he has to do! But he does it out of his heartfelt and authentic way of life. It's his own way of celebrating the festival of life. And he ultimately becomes a very unlikely 'leader': so many start following him in his run! He becomes an icon. It's because there is a sincerity in Forrest Gump. This basic sincerity also underlies the Buddhist search of the spiritual.

Several kings and several emperors used to come to Gautam Buddha. He used to teach them with very subtle examples: just through his smile, through his inner radiance, through a few words. He used to teach them how to lead with humility, and not just being madly in a race of being result-oriented. Numerous kings like Prasenjit (Pasenadi) were deeply influenced by him, and became great leaders in their own lifetime. Several renounced their old ways of leadership and improved themselves on that score. So too can we learn from the Buddha. It's about taking joy in the spiritual aspects of life, with a smile in heart and spirit, plus a tremendous dynamism in positively influencing self and others for 'real-world work' also!

CHAPTER- 7

Stop Fighting with Yourself

LESSON: Make peace within yourself. That is the first step to being truly effective and fulfilled in whatever work you attempt as a leader. The art of inner peace is in the Buddhist perspective a natural consequence of simply 'looking within', watching the flow of your emotions and thoughts but not identifying with them. This non-identification with our inner conflicting thought-impulses leads to a spontaneous inner peacefulness. It is the very crux of the Buddha's meditative process.

In the Buddhism of Tibet, it is said that if a person does not stop fighting with himself, there is no hope of moving towards any evolution. The whole understanding is that the human being wants to fight—whether with others or with oneself. And neither way does any peace come to us as human beings. So the impulse to fight is something which is really at the heart of destructive behaviour. It does not mean that you are not to have courage, it does not mean that you become afraid to fight for the greater good when necessary. That is not the thing; the whole essential thing is that you do not carry on fighting with yourself. Because in that way, you never attain the clarity required to be a good leader or in fact to be a good human being.

In Japanese culture, deeply influenced by the Buddhist point of view, the samurai warriors were taught that they are to win the battle within themselves before they can defeat others! And you can only win the inner battle by stopping the impulse to fight within your consciousness, getting rid of self-conflict and worry. Then your action in the outer world become dynamic, becomes non-destructive, becomes full of grace. And you do what has to be done in a manner which is free from unhappiness.

You can choose the kind of leader you want to be. You can be a happy leader or you can be an unhappy leader. Happy leaders will create happiness for the people they lead, and unhappy leaders will create unhappiness for the people they lead. It's very simple. If within yourself you are unhappy—by constantly fighting yourself and being not at ease with yourself, but in a constant tension—

then you cannot expect to be a leader who is happy. So then, how can you expect your leadership to have happy results?

Buddhism believes that the subtle is always stronger than the gross, meaning to say that the spiritual aspect of life is stronger than the material aspect. The unseen is greater than the seen. The consciousness is greater than the mind-body's actions. So, if at the level of consciousness you decide not to be in a constant state of anxiety—in other words, constantly fighting with yourself, at unease with yourself—then you cannot win with any kind of totality. You see, the usual psychology of man is to be a 'winner'. We are told about 'positive thinking', 'winning', 'how to win' and so on. But the whole spiritual point is that within yourself there is nothing to win! You are already a winner. So it's better to give up and surrender the fight, lose yourself in spiritual bliss within yourself. And when you lose yourself or surrender to this higher and greater mystic impulse, then you move towards attaining a true victory in all that you attempt outwardly.

In this context, we should understand one thing first: what is meditation (jhanna)? From the Buddhist point of view, it is basically becoming a witness to all that is going on in your inner domain of consciousness. And when you become a witness to this inner domain of consciousness, you will see a constant movement of thought—of anxious thought, one thought after the other, thoughts of desire, thoughts of acquisition, thoughts of violence, thoughts of fear. But the whole issue is, if you follow the Buddha's philosophy you come to realize that it's all about not participating in the fight of these thoughts going on in your head. Thoughts are at constant war in your own head, but you are not to fight them or struggle with them. You just let them pass. And so doing, you attain a victory over them. So the sense of being able to witness things, to be a silent witness or silent observer of the different fighting thoughts within your head, is what the Buddha's meditation is. That brings you to an inner peace. So essentially a leader also sometimes has to be a witness, to be able to step back and assess things in a broader manner. You are only able to do that if you choose not to jump into the fight. A lot of leaders do not really evolve or do not move to higher positions because they want to be 'street fighters' constantly. They keep needling their teams. Whereas a leader's real job is to be a guiding light. And you can only be a guiding light when you are a little detached from the fight itself. You can only be a pathfinder if your eyes are on the path, and if you are not constantly prodding and poking the people who are walking the path. Be a little detached from your thoughts, give up the fight of thoughts within your mind, and attain an inner peace. Attaining inner peace is the whole message of the Buddha. And it has practical sense for any kind of achievement we want to have in life.

If you look at people like the Buddha in a superficial manner, you could easily bracket them as being just impractical spiritualists. But the fact is the Buddha's philosophy is the most practical, because in one stroke it gives you the secrets about how to become fulfilled within your inner being and also about how to use this inner fulfilment for good and dynamic action in the world. Hence, it is tremendously important for the subject of leadership.

In the Western world particularly, there is a re-emphasis on simplicity in management, on simple actions for great effect, on clarity in thinking, and so on (several of these are based upon learnings that stem from profound Buddha-wisdom, whether we acknowledge that or not). Simplicity in mind leads to simplicity in action, but simplicity in action does not mean weakened simplicity. It means action which is clear-cut, filled with the energy of clarity. So, companies who wish to be lean companies, who wish to be dynamic, are moving towards simple structures, breaking down of hierarchies and so on. This has much to do with the inspiration which people like Buddha have infused into human consciousness: be simple, do not get involved in the rubbish of the thoughts which you are constantly fighting in your inner self. Give up that fight. Move away from it, and then you will emerge victorious through the peace you feel within. Charismatic people are those who have been able to create the state of grace, silence, peace within themselves. What is within themselves gets manifested as their outward charisma.

The whole idea of man's fighting is rather idiotic, because essentially you can't win the battle against life itself! All of us have to surrender to the fact of death. All of us have to surrender to the fact of being temporarily here on earth. So it's better in your mind to reconcile yourself to the limitations of material-physical human life. And the miracle is that when you reconcile yourself to the limitations of material-physical human life, then only do you emerge victorious in the domain of consciousness.

Buddha used to say that the ultimate truths about life cannot really be expressed in human language. This is very significant. What it means is that the truest things, the deepest things, cannot be measured by the barometer of man-made standards and material results, nor by language. It is the subtlety of life which is really the best and highest part of it, and it is through the subtlety of being that we evolve. In the world of the Buddhas, it is not the 'logic' of the words which is important, but it's about understanding that life is comprised of certain fundamental spiritual principles. If we understand these spiritual principles, we are able to function in a far more practical and forceful manner. Therefore, understand and imbibe the lesson of simplicity: it cuts out the unnecessary and allows the highest in you to shine forth within your life and leadership choices.

Over the centuries, Buddhist monasteries have been centres of great excellence and creativity. This applies to all sorts of monasteries: the monasteries in India, China, Japan, Sri Lanka, Cambodia, Vietnam and so on, each have had their own special interpretation of the Buddha's words. Each of them has also been able to come up with hugely creative arts, philosophies, and so on, and has had a deep influence upon human consciousness. If we can emulate and learn a little from these vast teachings, we will not only find the ecstasy within ourselves, but also find the joy and energy to function better as leaders within the world.

CHAPTER-8

Harmony Begins with an Inner State

LESSON: Synthesis or harmony of being is the root of effective and constructive action. Buddha's view of harmony begins with the purification of our thought processes: de-focusing from everything you have known, and relaxing into the limitless pure being that you are. This activates your highest consciousness and unused capacity for dynamism.

One of Buddha's most significant contributions to the world is his insistence that all harmony (the state of *samaggi*) begins with an inner *(antara)* state of being. Only through a state of peace, contentment, bliss, and fulfilment in the interior of one's being can one have the power to manifest creativity and productivity in the outer world.

This is a very important lesson as far as the subjects of success and leadership go. Usually we find individuals in leadership positions to be full of inner conflict themselves; in a lot of stress, anxiety, tension. How can one positively expect a harmonious outcome in the external world or the material world as a result of such leaders being in positions of power? They will only bring more and more conflict. They cannot create more harmony. It all begins in the inner state of our consciousness: this is an extremely important thing to understand. This is what makes the mystical or the spiritual aspect of Buddha's teaching profoundly relevant. It has implications not just at the psychological level, but in the very understanding of the vibrations which a leader must seek to create in the world.

So, eventually it comes back to a leader's spiritual roots: what state of being she or he is in. If a leader is functioning out of ego, she or he will only manifest ego-based conflicts within the world. So this is extremely important. If a person is disturbed in their inner being by small things, small discomforts, or stress and strain, how can she or he possibly create a better world or a better work environment? If a person is full of inner misery, how can they create outer happiness? We must think about these things, because essentially leadership is not just about the skill sets that we have. It is about the level of truth that has arisen in our own beings. It is about the level of joy that we experience in our own beings. Because eventually, that is what will show and express itself in the leadership style of the individual.

Several leaders are impelled by impulses which are not necessarily harmonious. In fact, quite the opposite. A lot of them have lost sight of what is important within themselves as human beings. Hence, whatever they do in their leadership positions does not really help the situation. It only aggravates situations. It only leads to more and more anguish and tension in their organizations or societies. Real positive transformation is a product of the empathy leaders can feel within themselves, the compassion and understanding they can feel. That is what it means to be a healing leader or a positive leader.

The world has seen enough leaders who have invested their energies in conflict. The next paradigm has to be of leaders who can heal the world, who can heal their communities and ecosystems in the best manner possible. And it all begins with the inner state.

Gautam Buddha usually did not speak on mundane and everyday things unless he was specifically asked for his advice. His concern was more about the domain of our foundational consciousness. If that goes correctly, everything goes correctly. If that is harmonious, everything becomes harmonious. But if that is in conflict, then only conflict can be the result.

Hence, we are to remember that as individuals, we should not cling to our negative states. The human mind has a very big attraction for its own negative states. It keeps clinging to negative states and enhancing them through imagination, increasing its effectiveness over us. And so doing, the conditions become right for creating outer conflict. This applies not only to leaders, but in our whole attitude towards success. The whole 'science of positive thinking' is a little shallow, because it takes away the power of doubt, it takes away the ability to question things. But what Buddha is talking about runs a little deeper. It is about seeking to bring your inner being into a state of harmony. And through that harmony comes bliss and happiness as a natural consequence, thereby whatever action you do has more of a capacity to create joy. And to be of real positive value.

Being a leader, or a successful person in any field, is ultimately all about creating value. But many leaders end up destroying value instead, being forces of value-destruction instead of value-creation. This is because their inner evolution is lagging behind their outward position of power. There is a big gap between what they are allowed to do in the world, and how their internal state is functioning. On the one hand, they have a lot of power. But on the other hand, within themselves, perhaps they are not functioning as smoothly or as harmoniously as they should be. So what happens is that their power of destructiveness goes up. They create conflicts within the workplace, within society. This is the root cause of the cumulative destructiveness we can see in all aspects within our beautiful blue planet earth.

Essentially, it is about creating a level of inner affluence. Out of inner affluence comes outer affluence. The way you feel deep within is really the vibe which is conveyed to the world. And that is what charisma is. Some people have a very joyful, enigmatic, magnetic charisma. This comes out of a state of inner affluence and creativity. And the beauty of it is, just by remembering that we are to be inwardly affluent and inwardly harmonious, our actions within the world automatically take on these qualities of harmony. It is like autosuggestion. Buddha used to say, 'You are what you think.' So if you imbue your mind with the thought that you are to be harmonious within, a beautiful journey begins. And you find that you are refreshed, reborn in your understanding of your own potential. You are able to enhance your capacity for harmony, instead of clinging to negativity. And from that point on, you become a far more positive, productive person as an individual and leader.

CHAPTER-9

Let Go of Enmity

LESSON: The Buddha's own life was a testament to the power of fraternal feeling and a universalistic view of all. That was why he could lead the single largest religious commune ('sangha') in history. It is the birthright of every being to be an equal citizen of this cosmos, yet to honour this birthright we must also reciprocate this similar vibe towards others. We must let go of all hatred and aversion: this frees us internally and dynamizes all our interactions. The greatest leaders know how to both give and command loyalty and fraternity, through the magic of convivial feeling.

"The fault of others is easily perceived, but that of oneself is difficult to perceive."
Gautam Buddha

One of the most profound principles when it comes to leadership effectiveness, is the ability of the individual to let go of personal dislikes. You see, the one thing which holds human beings back in their potential realization is the bondage of enmity, of animosity, of not liking others or getting along with others. This sense of enmity, once it is *let go of*, a person becomes truly free to be themselves. The burden is lifted! Your individuality comes to light. You can fly in the open sky without being weighed down by the sense of enmity.

Throughout his life, Gautam Buddha tried to make people bond in a manner where they would not be conditioned through personal enmities, but could go beyond it. In fact, there is an instance in his life when somebody spat on him, and his disciples were very angry with that person—some even wanted to beat him up. But Buddha just let him go. When asked what it was that allowed him to remain so calm, he simply said that it was his choice whether to react angrily or to react calmly. So he simply chose to react calmly. And this example has had a profound effect on people like Ashoka the Great. After the Kalinga war, Ashoka had a real change of heart. He learnt from the Buddha's mystical teachings these leadership attributes: of forgiveness, of compassion. Which is why he is always regarded as one of the greatest leaders who has ever lived in the world.

Now again if you look at the Bhagavad Gita also, you will find echoes of a similar teaching. Krishna tells Arjun to not have a personal enmity on the battlefield. The opponents are not to be taken as enemies but just as actors in this great play which the cosmos is unfolding before us. So too in the samurai tradition of Japan, which is based on the Bushido code derived from the Zen teachings of the Buddha, a similar principle is applied: the enemy is not an enemy in feeling nor to be personally disliked. If you carry enmity in your heart, you could be a powerful leader, but you will never be a satisfied one. There is another way of leadership: that is to be open, to be your natural self, and not always hyper-competitive with a sense of hatred or enmity. The other does not have to be 'defeated' for you to win. There is enough in the universe to make everybody a winner.

With this attitude is born great creativity. With this attitude is born great co-operation and teamwork. In fact, in the modern workplace this is very important because there is so much ill feeling between people in the same organization or nation or system. Because of this friction, a lot of destructiveness goes on. That same energy which can be utilized for good things and creative things gets lost in this infighting. So as a practical means of realizing the team's potential, it is imperative that the leader lets go of enmity, of dislike, of personal preferences, and allows herself or himself to instead be so liberal and free in their mindsets that they become catalysts for real transformation and creativity.

We are all part of the same cycle of existence. The tree gathers nourishment from the soil. The birds and animals find shade and fruit under the tree. Human beings gather the sweet fruit of the tree. And so on and on does the cycle of life move. Letting go of enmity simply means that you are becoming more and more a part of this cosmic cycle, this give-and-take between people, without getting identified with enmity. The tree does not discriminate between the different birds who come and sit on its branches. A leader in fact should be like a very strong tree, with deep roots, upon which a lot of people can rely and believe in. The great leader provides the necessary shade for others to grow and flourish in: she or he creates a mini ecosystem within which things thrive.

Letting go in thought is one of the most liberating factors in life. It simply means letting go of the mind's obsession with personal choices. Choices are good, but often our impulse is very conditioned by past thoughts: we are not open enough to co-operate with new people. And the leader of the future is one who can work well with new people, without having a feeling of animosity towards them.

This does not mean that the leader is one who is

lenient. In fact, it is quite the opposite. A person who lets go of negative energy gathers more authority and more charisma. And eventually is more listened to! The old way of leadership perhaps could have been to force people but this is an age of creativity. In this age of creativity, the courageous leader is one who has enough substance within oneself to be able to look past one's personal predilections, and to come to a place where he is able to trust others. Great leaders know what it means to trust human beings at a broader level. Trust requires letting go of distrust. And one's authority is not diminished by this. Instead, one's authority is enhanced, because one starts having real believers in what one is and what one stands for! The authenticity of a person is much easier to see in today's world. In many ways we are exposed in our world of today: through our interactions, through our mails, through our attitudes on social media. So it's better to be natural yourself yet without feelings of deep dislike towards others. That is just a conditioning which perhaps your education, your experience, or the society you live in has consciously or subconsciously burdened you with. Let go of it! And let the heart believe with a totality in your team, in the people you are working with. Then you will find that not only do you become more productive, but you become a natural leader and gain respect from your peer group too.

CHAPTER - 10

Dynamism Is Being Yourself!

LESSON: Unlock your greatest abilities by overcoming the mental weakness of imitation or trying to be like anybody else. Feel strong enough to be yourself! There is none like you and shall be none like you: each being is a unique product of the cosmos. Buddha urged his disciples to find their own truth in the most interior part of their own beings. Truly original, maverick, and transformative leaders have this authentic self-belief and self-drive: nothing else is fundamentally needed.

The thing about leadership is that somehow people are very interested in wearing masks, in not being themselves, in trying to be somebody apart from who they are. But this in the end is not a very good leadership strategy. Neither for you personally nor within the world. Dynamism is in being yourself. This has been a central message of Gautam Buddha. He used to insist upon being at your most genuine self, for there resides the potential Buddha or enlightened being within you.

And on the other hand—the practical side—it also does not make sense to *not* be who you totally are, to maintain a façade or wear a mask. Because the world now has become far more transparent. It's easier to read into people. We are almost exposed. So while wearing a mask for a leader is effective for a while, it is not ultimately fulfilling in any manner. The whole thing is to be in a state of being where you can be more of your own self, instead of trying to be like somebody else. That way not only are you able to integrate the wholeness of your own energy within yourself, but you are also able to genuinely share your energy—the best of your energy—with those you lead. That is what dynamic leadership is about, that is what truly positive leadership is about.

In Buddhism it is said that while being true to yourself may bring frustration or disappointment for a little while, in the end there comes about an organic and luminous quality within you. You become inwardly whole. You find the centre of yourself. And a person who finds the centre of himself has a very big impact on others. It creates a solidity of your personality, it creates an aura.

Eventually when it comes to the meditation which Buddha taught, it was all about being at your most genuine self. So your mind moves into a space where it is at one with what you *essentially* are. And that is the whole quest of meditation, that is the whole quest of spirituality. Never be afraid of being yourself with a hundred per cent of your being! That is what is needed for your true fulfilment and success. Your happiness depends upon how inwardly genuine you are. And it is extremely important for a leader to be in a happy frame of mind. Else what happiness can he bring? What value can he bring to his people, to his product, to the cause he serves?

The cosmos has created our life as we are: we don't need to be somebody else. The only limitation we have is that we have so much unexpressed energy of our genuine selves, that we become restricted and stifled. We withhold who we are, because we've been constantly told we should act one way or the other. Now, acting in a manner which is dictated to us—or which is told to us is the 'correct manner'—is not necessarily from our genuine energy. Hence, no great passion, no great love nor energy arises through such action.

Eventually, dynamic action is that which is imbued with your inner passion. The search for leadership excellence is always a search for passionate action. And passionate action can only take place when your inner being is integrated. Out of this integration comes about genuineness: being yourself, not being pseudo, not living in pretension. You see, the subject of leadership must deal with the subject of pretension: most leaders are trying to project, in smaller or greater measure, unconsciously or consciously, what they are not genuinely. This is a very common trait in leaders in various walks of life. That is why humanity in general has lost faith in its leaders! They don't seem very sincere; they don't seem very genuine. They just manipulate according to the situation. It is very rarely that you find a spontaneous person, whom you can trust in a manner which is complete. Whose very leadership vibe gives you hope and great trust, and relaxes you mentally. And it's only when you are yourself, when you are genuine, that you acquire an ability to command true trust. And out of this trust comes credibility for your leadership role.

Buddha used to say that there is great wisdom within us, but most of it we are not aware of nor awake to. And because we are often not genuine enough, we are not allowing this wisdom to flow into the actions of our lives. We are not being natural enough to allow this wisdom to flow. If only we can be our natural selves, if only we realize the seed of Buddhahood that we carry within, everything starts becoming luminous. Your very quality of consciousness then undergoes a great change. And with a change in the quality of your consciousness, you become ready for greater things in life.

Being genuine is like going back to the source of yourself. When you go back to the source, there's a different bliss and a different fulfilment. In India, the source of rivers was always considered holy. That is true for the Hindus, the Buddhists, and all the religious or pagan paths also! The source of the river is important! What it really means is that you have to go back to the source of yourself: that place from where the inner Ganges starts. It is a metaphor: go back to your original being, your genuine source of self. There is the temple, there is your life-force, and your inner fire. There is your true, genuine power.

Being dynamic means reconnecting with your inner light. When you reconnect with your inner light, you're able to shine its power into the world. Go back to the flame of your being, that which is your very spirit and essence! That flame of your being has the power to burn all negativities down, leaving you pure. Energized! Finding the glory of all your inner energies, feeling strong and genuinely powerful in your original being, ready to take on the world! That is what happens when you are prepared to be yourself completely and genuinely. That is not only beautiful, but also ultimately the secret of all true abundance in life.

CHAPTER - 11

Trust Your Own Experience

LESSON: Buddha taught his disciples to go by their own authentic experiences only, and not just trust scriptural or dogmatic advice! And that is the key differentiator between excellence and mediocrity in any field: spirituality, science, business, art, technology, etc. The real pathfinders and breakthrough leaders within any field depend upon no established knowledge but rather take a great leap into innovative thought/action, relying on their own insights. You can observe this principle: true leaders inculcate it within themselves and empower their teams to do likewise, thereby leading to something new, creative, advanced!

The whole basis of Buddha's teaching is that it is your own experience which matters: there is no question of a 'belief system' within Buddha's core principles! 'Belief' can be of many kinds: belief can be in our knowledge, our education, our ideology, our religion, our sense of nationalism. But eventually, all belief is misleading. Buddha does not allow any shortcuts in one's pursuits. He says to trust your own experience because that is the most direct way of knowing truth.

From the success and leadership perspectives, this is really essential. But why? Basically because a leader is to be fresh in perception, and not be burdened with the baggage of certain concepts, the baggage of certain ideologies. But the opposite is in vogue today: you can observe it in world leaders—they have so much investment in belief systems, that they are not able to move on to the new. They are not able to be creative and innovative. The whole creative and innovative spirit needs your consciousness to be absolutely free of the encumbrances of acquired knowledge. Then is your consciousness in a state of readiness for fresh perception.

All the mavericks of the world, the path-breakers, the leading lights, were people who freed themselves from established thought systems, from religious dogmas, from the cages of ideologies.

This basic principle applies to every aspect of life. You can see it in the business world. This is an age of disruption. This is an age where old models will not work in the present-day business scenario. So what is the leader to do? A leader first of all has to let go of that which has been known in the past. That is the first step. Only then can the new enter. Only then can innovative leadership play its part more and more.

As we progress as a civilization, we come to see that it is truly innovative and creative leadership which is effective: Elon Musk for example, or Steve Jobs. People who can think beyond the established box. But the essential basis—the spiritual basis—of it is that they believe and trust only in their own experience, their reading of situations. They do not work out of jaded, old thought models. Originality is real wisdom. Wisdom is not acquisition of knowledge. Wisdom is the ability to keep your consciousness so clear and so broad in its scope, that it is never caught in the prison of the known. And when it is not caught in the prison of the known, then it is powerful. It is capable of joining concepts together, joining people together, inspiring teams, and so on and so forth.

So, this is the very root, the fundamental way of understanding: that it is one's awareness of the experience which is important. That experience could be of any kind. It could be one's reading of society if one is in politics. The astute leader in politics is one who can be conscious of the originality of his own reading into things, in order to create a new path ahead. She or he can then be a pathfinder in that field.

The problem is, leaders are always tempted to fall back on tried and tested ways to guide people. But in today's world, that is not working! People are becoming redundant as we move towards artificial intelligence. That is why the teachings of Buddha are so important, because he talks about the basic consciousness and the quality of consciousness. If that is alright, one's journey on the path ahead spontaneously becomes free of danger. One is able to climb the peaks of attainment. To climb higher, you need to shed baggage. That is the way of the Buddhas. Otherwise you'll never be able to reach the summit of the mountain.

As a leader, you are to leave aside the overdependence on the logic of the past, which has been handed over to you as part of your education, as part of your training. The very word 'training' is almost antithetical to what the Buddha preached: no amount of training can make a person have insight. And insight is the real quality of leadership. A good leader is one who can have such insight into things, that whatever he touches gets imbued with a new aspect. That is leadership vision: to bring in something original of yourself. And to bring in something original of yourself, all you have is your own experience, not acquired 'knowing'. So it's a quality of your awareness which is important.

Shine your own light unto situations, and see with fresh eyes what they are. Then you become capable of being dynamic, being supple and flexible in your mind. Suppleness and flexibility of mind leads to an enhanced problem-solving ability. This should be the attitude. You cannot really lead or help others if you yourself do not have insights into things. And true penetrating insight can only be developed when you destroy that which you carry as mental baggage. Then only is your mind fresh.

In Zen Buddhism there's a concept of the 'fresh' mind, the 'new' mind, the 'beginner's' mind. It is the mind which is so fresh and responsive in its immediacy of understanding, that it reads deeply into situations with great speed. And reading deeply into situations, there comes the ability to find something new, something creative, to solve the problem or innovate a new product, and so on. At Apple Inc., the whole basis of aesthetics is based on Buddhist teachings (particularly those which comprise Zen in Japan). Steve Jobs was so deeply inspired by Zen aesthetics and philosophy, that he brought its simplicity of character, its freshness, into creating Apple Inc. And Apple Inc. is arguably one of the most successful companies of all time. Steve Jobs is of course one of the most revolutionary leaders of all time too—not only a thought leader, but a person who transformed the world of technology itself, and in the process created a great example of what creative leadership is.

So, Apple is the most profound example in the business world of seeing Zen Buddhism's philosophy in practical action. But there have been several others also. Larry Brilliant who heads google.org (the philanthropic arm of Google) was also deeply interested in Indian mysticism and spirituality, and out of that came his vision to transform people's lives through service, as the Seva Foundation and other organizations. Ergo the Zen philosophy works, whether for product innovation, technology leadership, or leadership in business philanthropy. There have been so many who have combined not just business acumen and leadership, but the ability to create something fresh, something new! At the root of it, several times, have been Buddha's profound insights.

How You Live Matters, Not What You Desire

LESSON: Transform your energies by shifting them from their investment in egoic desires, towards creating a spiritual quality or vibe of meditativeness within yourself. This creates mental quietness, heartfelt joy, and a greater capacity for value-creation and abundance-creation as a leader in your own field.

The whole insistence of the Buddha was to create such quality in life that every moment becomes luminous with grace, with consciousness, with bliss and joy. Not only for oneself, but for others also. That is the whole concept of the Bodhisattva: living each moment in a manner which is ultimately fulfilling for one's entire ecosystem. Isn't that what leadership is meant for? To create such moments for one's self and for others. This leads on to a greater quality of life, a 'light' within the being, and ultimately to a greater abundance of living for all.

It is not about personal desires. In fact, Buddha constantly points at desire as the most pernicious thing, which has the potential to destroy the quality of life within the moment. Now, desires in themselves are not at fault, but our *obsession with desires* is what takes us away from our roots. So, Buddha's view is the alchemy of inner change, within your inner world. You are to become abundant deep within. Make life a success within yourself, and then you become capable of making your leadership position, too, more successful. Do so in a manner which is not about ego, but is about creating a living quality of grace for everybody you lead. This requires a mind which is very open. This requires a mind which is not imprisoned by more and more desires. This requires a mind which has discarded its burdens and pretensions and is no longer deceived by the constant cycle of desire. Instead, it has thrown out unnecessary things—ego problems, anxiety—leaving it with a quality which is completely open to life. And this quality of openness actualizes our human potentiality.

In Buddha's time, joining his 'sangha' was said to be like a rebirth of oneself. It was simply about catalysing the alchemy of transformation within oneself. Giving 'birth' to oneself anew, and beginning a new kind of life within which *the way you live* becomes more important than a future goal. So too, in leadership: to lead well should be the aim and not just meeting goals. That will happen spontaneously if the leadership and team ethic is strong. Desiring and attaining the *position* of leadership and desiring the *results* are not the most important thing. It is what you do as a leader and the way you play your role that matters. That brings transformation. This teaching also reflects Krishna's teaching of Karma Yoga (the spiritual philosophy of work) to Arjun on the battlefield, in India's great epic the Mahabharat: it is about playing our part to our best, doing our dharma and then the results come—there is no need to obsessively desire results. So the *quality* of leadership transformation—and not desiring the fruits of it—is what it means to become a dynamo, a tremendously forceful leader.

It's eventually about creating an optimism within every moment that you exist. If you create this optimism, then only do those you lead become optimistic. And optimism requires a freshness of mind, a freshness of heart and of hope. Hopefulness is not about wishful thinking but is about creating a situation where your inner being is lit up with a quality of quiet inner confidence. Where it can celebrate its own consciousness, where it is not dependent on future results. This is again the message Krishna gives to Arjun in the Bhagavad Gita on the battlefield of Kurukshetra. It is the very core of the great epic the Mahabharat, and in a way summarizes the Indian approach to leadership: it is common to Buddhist and Hindu wisdom. The principle is: It is about *how* you fight on the battlefield, how you live, how you respond and react, which spontaneously creates a flow of leadership potential within you. People then automatically become inspired by you.

Hence, to be an inspirational leader essentially means to move your energy from desires to quality of consciousness. It's the same energy. The mind can either be living in a constant cycle of desiring, or it can be living in a manner which is alert from moment to moment. The mind should have the ability to enjoy simple things. Out of simplicity is born clarity. And clarity is one of the most important virtues for really great leadership. There is no substitute for clarity when it comes to good leadership. And how do you become clear? There has to be a space within you which is not imprisoned by desires—a space which is silent, a space which is tranquil, a space which is passive and ready for new things to happen. That is the basis of creative leadership.

It's about understanding that your effort as a leader should be one where you are completely involved in your endeavour in such a manner that future results do not disturb you. The thought of future results disturbs depthful perception.

We live in an age when it is constantly drilled into us that we must be better and better at what we do. But if you take a step back, you would find that it is not just being able to execute material things better which is to be the sum total of human living. In fact, it is more the ability to touch people's lives through your work, to be able to connect with people, to be able to experience a quality in your relationships (and in your relationship to yourself also).

Human beings are not 'things' or processes. We are organic wholeness. In Buddha's perspective, we are far more than we think we are. But we create barriers about ourselves, simply by being so full of *wanting things* that we do not pulsate with the wholeness of energy in the present moment. Dynamism and human excellence are all about pulsating with wholeness of energy in the moment you have right now. That will spontaneously lead to better results in the future. Hence, that must be the credo every leader—and every person pursuing success—should respect and understand, in order to enhance both their own lives and the quality of their leadership.

CHAPTER - 13

Be Blissful

*LESSON: In the ancient-most Buddhist vision,
one's true being is said to be of the nature of the cosmic
substratum or universal matrix: pure joy, delight, bliss.
Feel the vibe of utter and pure bliss within yourself:
that is real and direct meditation. In fact, it is the
only meditation really needed: it's not about sitting in
a posture and so on, but experience of a vibe within!
Thereby, you become capable of manifesting the quality
of bliss within all your worldly leadership roles. It is the
one quality that makes things meaningful: without bliss,
what is the point of anything? Purpose-driven leadership
is synonymous with blissful leadership: this needs to be
the new paradigm, echoing the ancient
wisdom of Buddhism.*

True dynamism comes from being blissful. Bliss, or *ananda*, is a very vital part of Gautama Buddha's entire teaching (one of his main disciples too, his closest one—his personal attendant—was also called Ananda!). Life is the art of ultimately knowing how to be blissful. And especially more so is this a virtue required for a leader. So we are to understand and delve deeply into the very basis of ananda: bliss, internal joy unlimited. It is the universal principle which governs all things, and is indeed very pertinent for leaders to understand.

All positivity, all hope, all sense of being *able to accomplish higher and vaster things* is a product of this innate quality of bliss or ananda. The leader should infuse this quality into his people no matter what the circumstances. The only way to live life at the optimum is to hold nothing back as far as the quality of bliss goes at first the individual level, and then at the collective level. It is a quality of the heart, but it enlightens the mind with a lot of courage. Otherwise we will just be in misery. You see, for a leader one of the most important things is to connect with people. But to be able to connect with people there must be a deep sense of blissfulness, a happiness in meeting others and reaching out to others. That is the very foundation for good leadership. Else we remain separate from people. Most people are not blissful enough, hence they cannot network and reach out to people in an effective enough manner.

So, the art of communication requires us to feel this bliss within ourselves. Only then do we feel like sharing things with others. What is bliss? Bliss is innate, according to the Buddha. It does not come from things. It does not come from objects. It is a self-luminous quality which is within you. It is not an externally created stimulus. It is the first experience of the truly mystical state. Bliss signifies grace, bliss signifies positivity and strength. A person who is blissful is like a magnet for others, because he or she exudes a quality which others aspire to. Every being in existence is looking for happiness, is looking for bliss in its own way. So, a leader who wants to be emulated must exhibit this feeling through his actions. Not in an artificial manner, but letting it arise through every pore of his or her being.

When it comes to work, the ability to be passionate at what you do also comes from bliss. Without it, there is no intrinsic love for the work. And without love for the work, there is no passionate energy being invested into the work. So while it seems an easy thing to remember, perhaps it is the most missed thing in modern-day leadership: the ability to be fully alive to all the joy you can harness within yourself. Then only can you begin creating a vibe which people are attracted to.

Buddha always says that it is our consciousness which creates our state of being. If our consciousness suggests to ourselves that we are depressed, we become more so. On the other hand, if you suggest to yourself that you are capable of great bliss and great happiness, it will start welling up more and more within you. The deepest founts of your being will open, and you find that you become more able to carry out tremendously great tasks.

Each being is carrying an unlimited fount of bliss within. But not very many channel this through their thought and action. We need to change our habit from looking at the negative to becoming more grateful for that which we have. Through gratitude can arise great bliss. Have gratitude for the position you are in. Have gratitude for all the things you are able to achieve, and not wonder about those which you have missed. Through this way, you start becoming more and more extraordinary. The one thing which people look for in a good leader is vitality: a sense of vital energy and inner integration. But all this is a by-product of the bliss the individual feels.

Modern-day society has attached so much importance to psychoanalysis that we start thinking we need help as far as the faculty of happiness and bliss go. But while depression is a clinical disease, by and large you will find people who have a choice about how good they are feeling. Most people become miserable out of choice. They do not enjoy their own beings as much as they can, and hence they do not tap into their innate powers. You have to feel the energy of bliss moving within you as a real thing. Then, automatically you will relax. But at the same time you will become more and more exuberant in action. People will be able to sense your energy.

What bliss does is, it changes the way you speak, it changes the way you walk, the way you shake another person's hand and so on. All this verbal and non-verbal expression is what goes into making a great leader who she or he is. Bliss is a foundational determinant of our very behavioural patterns as leaders and example setters. Hence, if you want to be a positive leader, this is the one quality you must look to do and not get entangled within your anxieties. Untangle yourself from the negative; and once you untangle yourself, there is nothing to stop you from being more and more strengthened with the clarity of bliss.

What bliss does is it gives you great mental clarity. The inner centre of you starts opening up to the infinite. Otherwise you remain closed. Anxiety closes you, shuts you out from better possibilities. You can see it in the body language of people. People who are feeling anxious close themselves up, crouching into themselves. It is only the blissful person who is able to be in a natural openness. Blissful people exude a very strong openness in non-verbal communication: as if ready to embrace the world. This natural openness of being is attractive to people. This creates a renewed self-confidence in you, and this confidence is communicated non-verbally to others. People start believing you more as an individual.

Bliss is an intrinsically individual thing. It cannot be bought yet it can be inculcated within you. It is eventually the highest form of meditation. The old Indian mystic mantra *sat-chit-ananda* means truth-consciousness-bliss. In the mystic view, bliss is the ultimate goal of all things: for the universe, for man, for humanity as a whole. It should be the aim. And if bliss is the aim, everything else which happens can be handled with ease. Otherwise we become depressed and anxious even about small things.

So, let bliss be paramount in your consciousness, because then only do you rise above the average being into real excellence. Being above average or excellent at work and in life is really a question of the amount of energy you can imbue into your tasks. When your energy is ecstatic, nothing can stop you! This ecstasy of feeling within your work, within your relationships, within your networking, is what bliss is about. And ecstasy therefore is the aim—or should be the aim—of a leader. Be ecstatic in what you do. Then does your energy explode into greater experiences, into greater achievements and higher excellence.

Positive Self-Esteem Vs. Destructive Leadership

LESSON: Gautam Buddha tells us that there are great depths of energy and self-power within us. And when a Buddha vouches for such things with authority, it is imperative that we make the effort to seek out these hidden depths within ourselves. Out of the discovery of inner richness arises real self-esteem and respect for all that one has been endowed with in one's inner core. Great leaders realize the sanctity of their internal energies, and utilize these beneficially.

One of the most important qualities for a good leader is to have a sense of positive self-esteem. Otherwise leadership can become very destructive. A classic example is that of Adolf Hitler: having been rejected by art school (he had wanted to become an artist), he lost self-esteem and his whole mind turned destructive. His whole sense of self became based on a very negative ego. Because of this innate problem that he developed, he became destructive in the world. Because something negative happened in his consciousness, he also manifested great negativity in the world. This affected millions upon millions of people, putting the world into a war which was unmatched in its destructiveness and evil. Having positive self-esteem is really the essence of good leadership. Spiritually, it means seeing the higher aspects of self. Gautam Buddha's message was to make people recognize their higher 'Buddha-Nature' or *Buddha-Dhatu*. We must in our own lives and leadership roles cultivate a sense of our higher selves and act through that, seeing the highest natures of ourselves and acting on those positive impulses instead of negative impulses. Buddha tried to make people see their self-power *(bala)* in a positive manner. He constantly reminded them that within them was the seed of infinite goodness *(kalyanata),* infinite virtue, infinite Buddhahood. And from this very seed comes positive self-esteem.

So, it is about the seed of consciousness which a person manifests. Look at the example of a tree. Whether the tree will bear poisonous fruits, or fruits that are sweet, fragrant, nourishing, is dependent upon the seed. Buddha's effort was to create more and more virtue within the seed itself. If the quality of the seed is good, it will sprout in a creative and productive manner. It is this very seed-level work which is the most important aspect of Buddha, as far as the material results of his work go. Because essentially, what he did was try to make people constantly aware that they could be a great source of goodness within the world, not only for themselves and within their own beings, but also manifesting it as positivity in the world. What it essentially requires is a sense of wakefulness to one's infinite higher qualities.

The mind is a very strange mechanism. It starts believing in things that are suggested to it. The mind gets conditioned by autosuggestions. And if the quality of the suggestion is negative, then gradually the mind becomes negative in its outlook and actions. So it is addressing this quality of self-suggestion that makes all the difference between whether a person will be a positive force of good in the world, or a destructive one. But essentially it is also about not being too oriented with the mind, because the mind keeps on throwing up negativities. It keeps on suggesting and exaggerating the negative aspect of life. So, Buddha says to go beyond the mind. Buddha says that our highest quality is beyond the conscious mind. You can call it the super conscious mind, you can call it the voice of conscience, you can call it the cosmic voice or the cosmic mind. Buddhahood is becoming one with this cosmic mind. That is the quality which allows you to transcend your self-limitations, and that is the quality which imbues you with a deep positive self-esteem. Because it does not identify with problems, but with the root of what you *are*, which is infinite bliss.

When the mind is relaxed, natural, and pure, then it has the ability to become very dynamic, forceful, energetic. Out of this dynamism, force, and energy comes about a great presence of virtue within your being. Others start feeling it too. Your being then acquires a vibe of palpable, charismatic power. You are then no longer stumbling within the mire of the mind and its pool of thoughts, but are alert and awake to a higher self within you. And it is out of this higher self that higher achievement can truly come about!

Deeply inspired by Buddha's *dhyana* or jhanna teachings, Chinese Buddhism says it's always a question of what you identify with that determines your level of fulfilment within the world. If you identify yourself primarily with your mind and thoughts, you may remain miserable. But if you identify primarily with your higher nature, you suddenly find an effortless, powerful energy in the way you function! That is what a leader should be doing: identifying with his or her highest energy.

Buddha taught evenness of temperament, as that is reflective of our higher nature. Now, good temperament depends ultimately upon your sense of self-esteem and has a big part to play in the way people perceive you as a leader. Ill-tempered leaders are tolerated for a while, but if a person is in a habit of being ill-tempered, they start becoming unbearable. Anger when it comes to work or achieving a task is often tolerable, but to have a consistent temperament of cynicism is the most destructive aspect that you can manifest. It is certainly not reflective of your higher nature! Hence, avoid being like that. The whole thing is in knowing yourself to be much more immense— much greater—than the *mood* you are in. Moods come and go, but if you identify with your higher nature, you remain unaffected by these. Even in a moment of anger, realize that the spiritual being within you is beyond the anger! And so doing, you start manifesting positivity. Through this, not only are you transformed, but your ability to touch others through your work and presence is, too. Your ability to influence others in a positive manner is enhanced, and essentially that is what great leadership is all about.

CHAPTER-15

Go From Thoughts to Awareness

LESSON: Buddhahood stands for pure awareness.
Several people think Buddhism is about 'sorrow'.
But it is, in essence, about the awareness that if we
keep investing ourselves only in outer pursuits, there is
only sorrow, while if we work on our inner awareness
happiness comes naturally. The boundless search for
the infinite part of being is the core of Buddhism.
Focus on that, and not on passing thoughts. The very
focus on generating greater awareness within yourself
leads to higher intelligence, energy, dynamism, courage,
and wisdom in the face of all life's problems
and questions.

The way of the Buddha is not in thought
(*chinta*), it is in awareness (*chetana*). This is the

key to understand, in order to manifest good 'leadership presence' through one's persona.

Reliance on the mind's thoughts is not very sound from the Buddha's perspective: mind being an instrument of perception, it throws up several things which are not necessarily true! Therefore, if we start believing in it wholly, we go further and further away from our self-truth and the truth of the universe. The way of awareness is to untangle ourselves from the limited thoughts of the mind, and become rooted in the truth of life with choiceless perception, without the interference of constant thought. This brings clarity, this brings the experience of attentiveness. And through the action of attentiveness, our intelligence and insight expands. Therefore, attentiveness is absolutely essential for leaders. It determines the power and effectiveness of your personal leadership presence.

Leaders often get entangled in anxious thoughts, but the way of clarity requires a remembrance of your essential being—the understanding that you are *not* your thoughts, you are *not* the biophysical mind and body. Once that realization is established in you, your energy becomes hugely empowered to perceive things as they truly are, and not the way your thoughts are suggesting.

Awareness is something which is at the heart of the spiritual and mystical search (you can find this echoed throughout eastern mystic paths especially). Especially so with the Buddha: his entire path is about patient awareness. And that is what leaders must cultivate more and more within themselves—patience to see that you are not the mind; patience to see that everything in the universe is simply a divine play which is going on, but which your mind is interpreting and twisting in a way that you lose this sense of play. You become over-serious. And when you become over-serious, both—the lightness of heart and the energetic freedom of mind—get taken away. And you begin taking wrong decisions for yourself, and as a leader you move into taking wrong decisions for those you lead. Awareness implies enjoying the moments of life through an absorption in what is happening, and not an absorption in the mind's thoughts, perceptions (which are often wrong), and imaginings.

Buddha used to say that the mind plays tricks on people; it can be an illusion-creator. It gives rise to imagined phenomena within the psychological and emotional planes, thereby deeply affecting the behaviour patterns of humans at all levels of their being. The mind often wrongly interprets things. Yet the whole focus of modern man lies in thought: we become so identified with our changing thoughts that we react according to them. These kinds of reactions—based on constantly changing thought perceptions—is what eventually leads to self-conflict, and to conflict between people. Most leaders are too defensive about their own point of view and their own thought; awareness means being open and accepting about other views. To be a good leader who can inspire people to work with co-operation, towards working well together, needs open awareness more than closed thoughts. For example, let us examine a crisis situation. Leaders of all kinds face crisis situations. It could be a crisis facing a nation. It could be a crisis facing a company or an organization. The essential thing is, how does the leader deal with the crisis? Here is where the part of the Buddha is very important, because he addresses the core issue of consciousness. If the consciousness is in a good, open state, the leader can solve the crisis in a far more aware and complete manner. Otherwise the leader is often too closed with his point of view, and in too much of a hurry to press that point of view, thereby making mistakes.

Essentially, the greatest ability of good leaders is the ability to establish deep contact with others. Through this establishment of deep contact with others comes about depth in relationships, bonding, teamwork, and so on. It doesn't matter whether this contact is at the level of a business network, or at the level of politics: it is all about making a heart-to-heart contact with people. Now, here again it is very important that we understand how thoughts can interfere and impede with this heart-to-heart contact. When a lot of us meet people, we have too many preconceived notions, or we judge people on one factor or the other. And this very judging of the mind sometimes makes us miss something more valuable. It makes us miss a warmth which can flow from one person to the other. People have become so head-driven and calculative that the human spiritual touch sometimes goes missing in relationships. But charismatic leaders know how to utilize this impulse of the higher spiritual nature in man. It's not about mental judgment and calculation alone. Yes, of course mental judgment is required: it's what keeps us safe from dangers and helps us survive. But leadership should be about more than survival. The whole point is that to grow into relationships which are important to you, the quality of heartfelt awareness is infinitely more powerful than the quality of the mind's changing thought-impulses.

One of the most important things for leaders to understand is that a lot of their energy is wasted in the meaningless confusion of thoughts. Eventually, the most effective leaders are they who are not fighting within their own thoughts, who are reconciled and peaceful within their own selves. Because through that, you are able to function in a far more smooth manner. Ultimately, the quality of leadership and of how you *feel* while leading is very important. You should feel that you are in a smooth flow. Therefore, learn to leave the heavy burden of thoughts aside sometimes. Just be yourself by going beyond thoughts. Invest in openness and awareness. And then you find that things can function far better. The flow of your being can function with far more energy.

With this feeling in mind and with this understanding, you suddenly realize that the tiredness, frustration, or expectations of leadership start evaporating. You become far more patient, and clearer. In that way, you are able to function to a degree which brings a great deal of focus and concentration to the tasks at hand.

The Only Thing which Is 'Yours' Is Within You

LESSON: Nothing can bring contentment apart from the realization that your only treasure is within. Utilize it in a way that you feel oneness with the great energy of the universe. Detach yourself slightly from worries and problems: that is the only way the true light of your inner treasure can shine bright, making you respond to all of life's challenges with grace and depth. Feel connected to the very soul of the cosmos, the very core of universal existence. Its light shines within you. Work on making that endless inner light shine brighter. All peace, calmness, wisdom, and strength come from there.

Buddha used to teach that all that is eventually yours is what is within you, inside you. We own nothing else in the world. We can ultimately only have access to our own beings. Hence, all transformation must begin from there. No circumstance, no position can ultimately transform you. What transforms you in the world is your inner work. This is why the spiritual vision of Buddha is so important. When your inner state is intensified, your ability for potential realization goes up infinitely. He used to say that the problem is not that people find it difficult to become enlightened or to find their own Buddha-nature: the real challenge is the very *wanting* to access your Buddha nature, the very desire to move towards enlightenment. Very few people have that, and those who have that live intense lives.

This principle applies not only to the spiritual path, but it also applies to intensity of purpose in whatever we do in life. You see, a sense of purpose is at the heart of good work. But all great purpose starts from understanding that you are only that which you are within yourself. Everything else can be taken away from you. One day you have power, the next day you don't. One day you have a particular relationship, the next day you lose that relationship. But what is in you is yours. Therefore, work on your inner spiritual self to the best of your ability. That way you become a purpose-driven individual, someone who is not afraid to confront reality. And that is the basic ingredient of great leadership.

What constitutes great leadership? Great leadership

begins with understanding that while you are a very small part of this whole existence, you have the ability to work great things within it! That tremendous self-belief is what great leaders have! So it's a mix between a certain degree of humility along with the sense that your inner being can have *infinite* meaning. If you understand this, then what happens is that you come closer and closer to your own *unlimited* self. From there can flow your creative energy. And out of such a flow of creative energy comes about the flow of all worthwhile leadership attributes: willingness to be bold, to call a spade a spade, to have integrity, to fight for and defend the team, to call out mistakes—of self and of others—and thereby enable course correction within the team/set-up/organization/state/nation and so on and so forth.

Now, creative energy is a very interesting thing: it requires inspiration. Without inspiration, it does not really function properly. And the ultimate inspiration is realizing that you have a wealth of potential within yourself. Your real treasures in the world are those which are inner, not those which are outer. That is the key element for successful life, as it inspires massive courage to work within the world. So, the spiritual learning is that you simply understand yourself.

One of the biggest impediments to creativity at work, and to innovative leadership, is that leaders carry a sense of ego about the position they have. Yet with this feeling, that the only thing you possess is *within* you, that you possess nothing else, comes about a realization that everything else in your life—including your position—has been a fortunate play of circumstances. In this way, a gratefulness arises for the position you are in. You do not remain egoistic about it. Through this self-realization, your creativity is unleashed. You are then able to become a force of good for others. And that is what good leadership is meant to be: a force of good for others.

So, it is a very fundamental realization: non-possessiveness about position and power. But the opposite is often true in the world: people feel a sense of possessiveness about their power or position. That spoils their whole leadership functioning. Because then their leadership is motivated by a personal cause, and that very cause restricts them in their functioning. Learn to be of such inner freedom that the greatest aspects of your being can be revealed to yourself and to others. And when the greatest aspects of your being are revealed, you automatically become charismatic.

The secret of leadership charisma is to be able to seem effortless in your actions, and to be at ease with yourself. This creates an ease with others. And people are charmed by that. They are attracted to it. Great leaders have an ability to be friendly (not over-friendly), and they are able to reach out beyond their individual egos. Because they know that eventually it's all about relating to people. Eventually it's all about motivating and inspiring people.

Very few people actually have this leadership ability of friendly, egoless, effortless functioning. Most people become imprisoned by their own position, by their own sense of power. They are not able to utilize the wholeness of their energy. The energy becomes blocked with a sense of possessiveness of position. The free person is one who can flow with ease. And to flow with ease requires you to understand very deeply that nothing but your own inner being is yours. This has a very freeing effect on your consciousness, because it takes away the anxiety of protecting what you have. It takes away your defences. In that way you become brave. You feel you have nothing to lose. And when you feel you have nothing to lose, your energy is able to flow and function much better.

These are very foundational things, dealing with the mindset and consciousness which a leader should have. The Buddha always talked about the foundational aspects of being, especially in the realm of consciousness.

There are many schools of management which teach leadership, but the essential part of *consciousness* is missing in several of these leadership modules which are taught. Eventually, it is not about a set of talent or skill; it's about one's entire attitude towards life which determines the kind of leadership which one becomes capable of. That is why the Buddha is so important for leaders—and for all those seeking true success—to understand.

CHAPTER-17

Look at What People Are, Instead of at What They Have

LESSON: Buddhism has a very benign and gracious way of looking at fellow beings, as fellow travellers on a wondrous cosmic journey. Treat people with empathy and kindness, no matter what their 'worldly' stature, and it will echo back to you a million-fold. Never get fooled into thinking that ill treatment of people will bring you rewards. It is in fact what egoistic leaders do, and it leads to eventual spiritual misery for them as well as damage to the world. Look at your work as an opportunity to radiate and resonate good karma: that is the higher meaning of being a real leader and a truly successful human being.

Buddhism teaches to look at what people *are*, and not at what they *have*. This is a very fundamental thing for greatness in life and leadership. Mediocre leaders look at what people have: their position, their wealth, and so on. Great leaders have the ability to understand what individuals are, and that is one of their greatest strengths— to be able to recognize the inner being of a person, their essential talent. So, a leader is a talent spotter. But really what it requires is insight. It requires the ability to see beyond what is outwardly apparent. You see, all human beings have infinite potential, but a great leader is one who can recognize the uniqueness hidden in the infinite potential of the individual. And so doing, they're able to mobilize those people to their cause in the best manner possible. This is expansive leadership. This is what it means to have true intelligence as a leader. Because real intelligence is that which can pick out the subtle.

The gross is recognizable by everybody, but only those with subtle insight can pick out the inner quality of things. So, a good leader is one who can effectively put to use what individuals essentially are. And so doing, their approach becomes one of generating true value within the world. Because they are in a way able to unlock the other person's capacities, merely by recognizing it. If you recognize somebody's capacities, they themselves start becoming aware of it. Some people are not aware of their own capacities, but when they encounter somebody who seems to recognize what they have within them, that very recognition creates two things. First, it creates self-confidence in the individual. And secondly, it creates a great confidence and respect for the person who has been able to recognize who we are at heart! So a person feels more total when he or she encounters a person who can recognize them as they essentially are.

The spiritual way is to go past the boundaries of what a person has, and go into the very core of a person's true potential. That is the hallmark of a great team leader. This applies to all domains of life: the world of business, the world of sports, the world of art, music, politics, or any other field. The ability to recognize talent in a subtle manner is key.

This creates an essential loyalty also. You'll find some leaders are very natural in their approach with others. They relate to others in a very natural way. These are usually the same ones who are able to inspire people into being more of what they are. When you can create a team where people feel such totality of their own selves functioning within the team, their respect for the person who has catalyzed that feeling becomes greater.

In a way, the human journey on earth is a continual discovery of the hidden parts of our being. That is what potential-realization is. And that is where the question of leadership becomes one of having subtle dimensions. Those subtle dimensions are the ability, primarily, to go deeper into things and to see what others are at the core. Everybody does not exhibit this ability in equal measure; good leaders do.

Ultimately, leadership vision is all about team-building and organization-building. Some people are exceedingly good at building organizations, but if you look at their fundamental quality you will find that they're able to identify the right people to build the organization. They are in fact catalysts who are able to bring about a unity between talented people.

So, a leader is one who can create unity within the team. But unity only happens when there is a mutual respect of each other's talents. It does not happen if there is a hierarchy of ego. There can be a hierarchy of structure, there can be a hierarchy of position. But it should not be a hierarchy of ego. Everybody has a certain job to do. Somebody's job may be more cerebral. Somebody else's job may be more action-oriented. And somebody else's may be menial. But there has to be a mutual respect. The greatest leaders are the ones who lead by example: they're able to even inspire self-belief in the people who are doing the smallest job. Which is why you often hear of great mavericks and business geniuses who have not hesitated to do the job of the office cleaner also. This invariably raises their respect in the eyes of their team, if executed with authenticity. And through this respect—this keyword called respect—comes about loyalty, and a more conscious recognition of the person's leadership position.

Essentially, a good leader has crystal clear insight into other people, or at least that should be the endeavour. Crystal clear insight means being able to look within, not only at the exterior of others. Do not distinguish between people just based on their material attributes. Each person has a particular individuality. It is up to the leader to be able to harness the different human forces together and forge a winning team. Leadership is all about connecting the power of different elements and bringing them together. It is like various rivers going into one ocean: a leader is able to direct the flow of all these different talents and go into the same ocean (which is a metaphor for the objective of the organization or the team goal). When this happens, there's a great feeling of unity. When everything is moving in a certain free flow towards a common objective, with clear direction, is when you realize that the team is alive with energy. Then the objective of the truly great team does not remain a dream. It becomes transformed into a vision. The Buddha always insists that we are not to live in 'dreams': here dreaming essentially means looking at a phenomenon in a dull manner, with not enough insight.

Most people judge others in an external form. They are not able to reflect on others deeply enough. But people are moved by those who can reflect on them and recognize their talents. People respect those who can give them confidence in themselves.

The best way to give people confidence in themselves is to be empathetic to what they are within their own beings. If you can recognize it and put it into action, there is no greater service on earth.

A real team-builder is one who can allow others to shine bright to the best of their ability. The best team-builder is one who can allow the inner luminosity of individuals within the team to shine like a great treasure. And when everybody shines their light brightly upon the task, then naturally there is a great clarity of objective. There is a great coming together of positive energy. Then solutions can be found in a much better manner; the wheels of the team can move smoother!

The worst kind of leader is one who places an individual within their team into a task which they are not fit for. This is simply a fault of their basic misrecognition of people. So it is a question of consciousness: being fully conscious to what the other person is. That is what leads to harnessing the power of the various individuals into one cohesive wholeness. If a person has a particular power or a skill, you are to harness that power in a way that can create a sum that is larger than that of all the individuals put together, in a kind of compound growth.

Add together the different powers of each warrior or team player within the team, and create a powerful fighting force out of it. An effective force, a unified force, which can move smoothly towards its common objective.

Eventually, the teachings of the Buddha are extremely important for leaders because they tell us about things such as insight. Which comes as a result of deeply looking at phenomenon and people. The deeper you go, the more are you able to recognize the truth of yourself and of your fellow beings. And recognition of truth is the beginning of a beautiful, fulfilling journey.

Evolved and Futuristic Leaders Don't Get Narrowed by Narrow Definitions

LESSON: A key characteristic of the Buddha is broadness of vision. In order to be a true leader of vision, expand your consciousness of all things, instead of trapping it within confines. There are no limits to consciousness, just as there are no limits to love. Expansion of consciousness creates visionary ability within leaders, allowing them to glimpse beyond what others see. This allows them to become beacons of a better future.

One extremely important aspect of Buddhism is to make people develop a vast, universal, cosmic point of view. Buddha's disciples had to go beyond those 'narrow definitions' through which they knew themselves before coming to him: as belonging to a particular caste, a particular region, a particular religion and so on. They were to develop or expand into a broad worldview and view of 'self': much vaster and broader in its scope, periphery, or circumference than they had thought about previously. Buddhism was truly democratic and universal that way, especially during its earliest years. Through his personal example of inducting people irrespective of creed, Buddha set the perfect leadership template. It is something to learn from: the global, cosmic, universal point of view that a great leader must have. It is the key to true expansion.

The Buddhist concept of inner expansion is very simple: we expand and grow when we are deeply passionate about something which is *higher* than ourselves. The Buddhist idea is to develop a passion for higher truth, for purpose-driven work and so on, which goes beyond our previous definitions of *who we were or where we came from:* our parentage, our race, our religion, our nation, and so on. That is the way our mind expands. Ironically, in our world of today while we have become very globalized when it comes to communication, you would notice that a large number of people have become confined by dogmatic thinking when it comes to their communities and so on.

But that is not what a futuristic leader should be. The leader of the future needs to be somebody who looks at the world as an undivided whole; a person who does not confine herself or himself by definitions of country, by definitions of ideology or race, and so on.

Dynamic leadership for the future requires people with an expansive and vast vision. That only comes about when our consciousness is transformed into seeking something higher than that whereby we identify ourselves. We are all conditioned by man-made definitions of nation, education and so on. But never get narrowed by narrow definitions. Rather, expand as a human being. It is a fallacy to be defined by particular societal definitions; you are infinitely more. To be greater human beings requires us to transcend our limitations and reach out in our scope of ideation to the broader world, by expanding our own horizons. The world hardly needs leaders with narrow horizons. The need for the future is people who can work with a totality of energy, which unites people across borders and across psychological divides. Otherwise something within us gets held back.

People are often not total in their functioning because they are imprisoned by certain definitions of themselves. The way of spiritual integration within ourselves is to reconcile our idea of ourselves as being universal citizens. That is primary. With this cosmic point of view, we can step boldly out and share our greatest talents with the broader world.

There is a big lag between people's psychological evolution and the evolution of their knowledge. People have garnered more knowledge, but psychologically we often still like to 'belong' to a particular community. We get confined by ideas such as that. Now, while it is good to pay attention to our own culture or our own way of life, this often becomes a great dividing factor when it comes to human consciousness. In our own consciousness we can become narrow without even realizing it! And that is of no help as far as our inner fulfilment and potential-realization go.

From the point of view of mystical Buddhist teachings, there is no need to compare between people, between communities, between nations. These are concepts which have to bite the dust if humanity is to evolve. Mother Earth is our common home. This cosmos is our common home. That is also the way of an evolved leader, the futuristic leader.

Hence, you can clearly see that if you want to truly evolve as a leader, you have to de-attach yourself from narrow tags and definitions. Free yourself from man-made boundaries and ideas; these hinder your communication with others in one way or another. We can now appreciate that the problem at the psychological level of not having a 'cosmic vision' is that somehow we are always somewhat *distrustful of people who do not come from our similar background.* Our communication with them is often perhaps not as open and free as it should be. But a great leader is one who can communicate *across the board.* A great leader is one who can talk freely to everybody as if he or she empathizes and understands their background, their points of view, and so on. And that is the kind of positivity which needs to manifest in all sorts of leadership: be it organizational, business, politics, or any other pursuit known to us as human beings.

The truth of the matter is that for centuries (and indeed for millennia), man's mind has been repressed into thinking that it belongs to a particular sect, a particular nation. This conditioning has gone so deep within people that even otherwise intelligent people start believing that they *are* who they have been *told they are.* But remember, you are much more than what society tells you. You are part of the wondrous vastness which is the cosmos. And so knowing this, look at all things in a manner which allow you to grow both internally and externally.

Growth is always a product of freedom. The greater the space to grow, the more the growth will happen. Confining things does not allow them to grow. So if you have space in your consciousness—in other words, if you are not imprisoned by definitions of nation-state, race, religion, and so on—it becomes easier for you to grow. And great leadership is all about growth: self-growth as well as the growth of those you lead. Now, there is another kind of leadership that is negative. This brand of leadership thrives on dividing people more and more. It thrives on creating barriers between people more and more, on confining people to certain small ideologies and thoughts. But that is not the expansive and positive sort of leadership which the world needs. The earth does not become better through that, and neither does one's sense of individual achievement and fulfilment. What is really helpful for the individual is to not miss the broader dimensions of being. Be a citizen of the world in your mind. Then only is true creativity unleashed in you, free of the encumbrances of boundaries.

All that is valuable in life is found by overcoming the suppressions of the mind. And narrow definitions always suppress the mind. The way of the Buddha was to open people's mind to a degree where they realized themselves to be a part of the cosmic whole. That way, the whole energy of life can change. We become transformed, we become creative in vision, we become part of something much greater. From that comes great passion and great energy to achieve higher things. *And to move on into seeing that whatever we identified with was eventually not who we truly are.*

For these reasons, let us no longer look at the world through the keyholes of our various ideologies or dogmas (conscious or unconscious: hidden deep within our psychic conditionings). Let us step out into the 'open', as it were, and look at life in totality. For then do we move towards becoming more 'total' or whole as human beings, consequent to which we can go about becoming more 'total'/whole/well-rounded in our work as leaders in our own capacities or stations in life.

Ordinary Leaders Lead through Fear and Great Ones through Vision

LESSON: The greater the person, the less would she or he need to rely on fear. Remember this as a golden rule for spiritually evolved leadership. It is a key principle of Buddha's social vision.

"Since it is impossible to escape the result of our deeds, let us practise good works."
Gautam Buddha

It is the most basic human understanding that people lead others through fear or greed. This can be observed anywhere. You can look at religious leaders. You can look at leaders in the world of business. You can look at leaders in the world of politics. A lot of them use these two tactics: either they make people afraid of pain of some kind ('hell'), or they tempt them with some reward (pleasure, metaphorically 'heaven').

This kind of leadership is not visionary leadership. Now, Buddha's religion was revolutionary because it did not depend on the 'fear' of God. It only depended upon self-realization. That is why Buddha is considered revolutionary in his role as a spiritual leader. He moved away from the usual things which religion tells us: punishment and reward in the afterlife, and so on. Rather, he emphasized a very visionary breakthrough, which is the vision of self-realization and 'Buddhahood'. It implies being great in such a manner that your motivations are not based upon fear or greed, but in fact based upon something higher. And that higher thing can be called purification of vision (*ditthivisuddhi*).

All purpose-centred leadership is vision-centred leadership. It comes out of an experience of your higher self. This kind of leadership is rare: where through vision itself a leader can infuse enough inspiration in others to make them loyal to the cause. Or to make them follow their highest inspiration, in order to achieve a common perspective. A good example in the modern world of such a visionary is Elon Musk. He is known to be a leader who inspires others through a vision of something higher. It could be of colonizing Mars. It could be space travel.

It could be a world where all automobiles are powered electrically. His model of teamwork is one where people coalesce around the vision. They trust the vision, and this trust in the vision makes the leader extraordinary. This sort of leadership is not only imperative for the well-being of our future world, but for humanity today. In fact, there is no other way if we are to survive as a species.

We have seen enough of history where 'reward' and 'punishment' have been the carrot and stick respectively, which leaders have held out, be they kings, emperors, ministers and so on. The carrot tempts on the one hand with some reward, and on the other hand the stick is always available to beat people up in some manner or the other. But this only signifies a great lack of leadership vision. We need richness of leadership vision. Be an inspirational leader, to a degree where your ideas themselves are so enriched with power that they become a magnet for people to gather around and support you.

Make your vision one where people feel inspired, energized with positivity. The model of work in the future must be oriented toward human welfare. It could be in the form of goods, it could be in the form of services, it could be in the form of a noble vision. Inspire humanity at a psycho-spiritual level, and don't just play to their baser instincts. This is the spiritual approach. This is the mystical approach. Otherwise there is no need for the mystical or the spiritual: we can just behave as a species as we've always behaved. But that is not the point. The point is to function with the possibility of reaching to the very peak of your own potential. And through this possibility comes about the possibility of leading others also to their own peaks of potential. That is intelligent leadership, that is noble leadership. Where the leader's entire energy is devoted to a higher cause.

In Buddha's case it was self-realization or enlightenment *(sammasambodhi)*: knowing the truth of the self and of existence. At a more material and mundane level, a business goal of a leader could be to address a pain-point of a consumer, or of a group of people. As a political leader, it could be to bring about peace no matter what it costs to his position. And if through these positive impulses, one can create a vision, then that is leadership worth emulating.

In the practical world you'd see a lot of people have a mixture of both aspects, positive and negative. You look at a leader like Alexander the Great: his vision was extraordinary, he had the ability to make his army believe that he was unifying the world. So was Genghis Khan: he was telling the Mongolians that his vision is to unify the world. But the eventual result of it was that millions died as a 'vision' of their leadership. So it did not really work as an example to emulate. While they were successful in their own way, you could say that their ideas did not truly succeed in creating well-being of people. Similarly, even Steve Jobs was known to evoke fear in people, though of course he did not do anything as negative as these conquerors did. But the element of fear was always there. However, that was more because of the decision-making process that he had to make; it was not out of malice for anybody else. It was not out of wanting to destroy other people's lives. It was about clear-cut decision making and doing what is best for the business objective. To survive in the entrepreneurial world of technology is difficult, as is to create something tremendously new and innovative which captures the world's imagination, hence perhaps even his detractors forgave him. Because through his vision, essentially, he by and large positively *inspired* people. And it is no coincidence that Zen Buddhism has been the constant thing throughout his life: he was Buddhist in outlook. Hence, he is a good example to emulate. It does not mean that a leader has to give up being angry, or being strict. Being strict, structured, and disciplined are part of the process. It is like the Buddhist monks in the sangha: there were tremendous rules for discipline. There was tremendous structure, because structure sometimes helps the organization, and the individuals within the organization, meet the goal. Growth can happen more through structure, through an organized effort. So don't worry about structure. But the whole idea is, do not get bankrupted inwardly through utilizing fear and greed as the primary leadership weapons.

Everybody has something unique in them and most have the ability to share this uniqueness with the world. So, share your uniqueness of vision. Share it with more and more people, and you will find that people become attracted to it. There are enough people who will resonate with positivity if you are passionate about sharing a positive vision with them. Hence, it's just a question of reaching out. You don't need to invent a vision: it can be an extension of who you are. In fact, let it be that which you truly believe in. Think of the few things you believe in, make a list of them. Think of the values you believe in, about how you can make things better for people, how you can solve problems. Through this very process of noting down and journalling, your mind will open up with great clarity, and you'll be able to see that there are certain things you've thought about or talked about which can inspire others. And if you can inspire others, you spontaneously become a leader!

Leadership is all about inspiring others. So, be that extraordinary leader who inspires and motivates others through the nobleness of vision. Fear and greed only create trouble in people's minds, and they are in fact the tools of the neurotic leader. The neurotic leader is eventually never truly successful, because despite short-term success there is no peace of mind. And that is not the kind of leadership we should be looking at emulating. The great leader not only makes a better world outside himself in whatever capacity he can, but primarily also makes a better world within himself. This is to be remembered, and this is why Buddhist spirituality is so important for life and leadership success.

C H A P T E R - 2 0

Great Ideologies Can Lead to Great Confusion

LESSON: The Buddha's way is beyond ideas or ideologies. It is free, unlimited, and unbound. The very idea of Buddha's message is for us to fly free in the sky of self-realized clarity. In Buddhism's vision, all ideologies are simply a mental escape mechanism to avoid confronting truth face to face, boldly. The way of the Buddha is to be bold before all situations, directly facing up to them, with a serene and calm demeanour. This exemplifies the true way of the great warrior and the great leader.

The most commonly misutilized tool by international leaders is that of ideology. Especially in politics, throughout world history you can see that ideologies have been used to sell a particular leadership. That ideology could be Marxist, communist, capitalist, extremist of any sort, and so on and so forth. It's about selling the dream of a utopia. This is what Adolf Hitler did: he sold the dream of the Reich which would last a thousand years. You see, people get enraptured and entranced by ideologies. But eventually, it leads to a lot of confusion because there is no final solution! There can never be one. Actually, every ideology in a way promises perfection, but always fails in achieving perfection, simply because we as human beings are not perfect.

Gautam Buddha never believed in ideology. Quite the opposite, in fact! Yes, he gave His disciples a 'structure' to follow: that of meditation and so on. But never overloaded them with ideologies, dogmas, or conditionings, as that would have defeated the very purpose of the monastic order or sangha: a place where the disciples moved towards ultimate enlightened freedom and not remain encumbered by 'rules and regulations'. This is in fact true of all original 'mystic religious paths': it is only much after their founder-visionaries died that religions sought to retain control over their followers by enforcing strict ideologies or ideas upon them. But it is always good for a leader—no matter whether he is a business leader, thought leader and so on—to be a person who does not use ideologies however 'great' they may initially seem (if he is to be honest, if he is to be truly of value in the long term). Instead, it is the *enduring values* which have to be emphasized. For example, the value of courage. Now, the value of courage does not belong to any particular 'ideology'. It can be called a basic humanistic virtue. Buddha used to say that courage is one of the primary things required for a person on the path: whether a person is a warrior or a householder, a businessman, a leader in the political sphere, or a monk. Courage is essential. Courage cannot be called an ideology, rather courage is a basic human virtue. *So, always choose human virtues and not ideology.*

The pernicious thing which ideology does is that it inflates the ego of the followers apart from the leaders. They start feeling great just by belonging to a particular community or circle. But they don't realize that they are being burdened with something which is artificial. What really helps humanity is the ability to work with ease with others. And in order to work with ease with others, we must drop ideologies. Otherwise there is only conflict. Now, how do you work smoothly with others? You can do so when you put your individual ideologies aside, and concentrate on human virtues. And together as individuals, you join your virtues as a team and then you move toward fulfilling a plan.

Each human being brings certain virtues to tasks. Emphasize those instead of fighting over differing viewpoints. In today's world you can see politics being discussed in every business organization, in every school, in every educational institution. This has led to a situation where people have become very tense with each other. People are not relaxed with each other. They do not work easily with each other, and that creates a problem with teamwork. Team tasks suffer. Team-building is all about making people at ease with each other. Therefore, it is imperative for humanity, for the organization or institution to emphasize not the neurotic obsession with ideologies, but enhancing natural communication between people. Natural communication between people is what is healthy. It's what creates a normal and natural society. What is abnormal is a society which is split between different ideologies and clashing all the time based on differing viewpoints. That never works. It only creates more and more confusion and imbalance. Even within one organization you can see imbalances.

The main problem between people is that they think their ideology is different from the other person's. It could be religious, it could be in terms of politics, it could be in terms of economics. But that is no reason to fight. There needs to be an ease within the collective, then only does the collective move well towards a collective goal. A leader is somebody who facilitates the meeting of a collective goal with as much ease as possible. He or she facilitates and ensures that the wheels of the organization run smoothly, and not get blocked again and again by people's clashes within it. In today's world, the religious believer cannot stand the atheist, the communists cannot stand the democrats, one religion cannot stand the other. So where is the room for co-operation, and for meeting common human goals? Which is why so much tension, anxiety, a willingness to fight and struggle with each other is manifested on earth. And in that manner, society goes on absorbing the wrong things. The inner impulses of people get affected.

Our inner impulses and feelings are very important when it comes to working as leaders, but also when working within teams. If the quality of the inner feeling is good, then all our other problems can be solved. Then together we can move like a great wave. Making people find common ground is a very vital part of the whole leadership exercise. Why was Buddha's monastic order so successful in its initial years? It was because he was able to create this ground of trust between people. He was followed by thousands upon thousands in his own lifetime. In that way maybe he's been the most successful individual spiritual leader ever, because in his own lifetime he had a massive following. Even emperors and kings used to follow him. Sadly, several years after his death the clashes started happening between the different Buddhist sects, based on differing ideologies. And the whole sangha got split. So it is a good example of what happens when people forget about their common ground, the common basis, and instead start arguing about small differences in ideology. These small differences turn out to be very important, destructive, and big. A good and positive leader is one who emphasizes common ground, and not differences. The negative leader is one who keeps emphasizing the differences between one and the other, because that may be played to their agenda of 'divide and rule'.

Essentially any team or society is to be looked at like a forest. All different sorts of trees can grow in the forest. Each tree is not the same as the other, but what is common between them is the common ground—the earth—they are all rooted in. They absorb the same water; they absorb the same sunshine. So, a leader facilitates this common ground. That is key. Eventually, what it means is that ideology can often be a bondage: sometimes instead of illuminating and enhancing people's potential, it stunts and retards it. The whole idea is that leadership should bring about positive growth, and to bring about true growth and maturity is required a vision where we realize we are connected and linked together. Creating linkages between people—and a feeling of being connected—is the very basis of great leadership. It is the essence of the Boddhisatva attitude, with implications for us all in our life and leadership roles.

Acknowledgements

I wish to express my humble gratitude to the people who have made this series possible:

Anuj Bahri, my super literary agent at Red Ink.

Shikha Sabharwal and Gaurav Sabharwal, my wonderful publishers at Fingerprint! Publishing and their team.

Garima Shukla, my amazing and brilliant editor.

Family—my parents, partner Sohini, sister Priti, nieces, nephews, et al: you are my rock.

Gratitude also to my support team, friends, mentors, and well-wishers over the years.

Pranay is a mystic philosopher. He is an expert on Indian and world spirituality.

Pranay's modules on 'Advanced Spirituality for Leadership and Success' (PowerTalks/MysticTalks for public and corporate audiences) have won global acclaim.

Pranay is also a theatre personality and playwright. His original productions such as *From Kabir to Kavi* and *Soul Stir* have been acclaimed by world luminaries for their path-breaking spiritual content.

Pranay and his partner Sohini run the socio-cultural philanthropic commune TAS, whose initiatives such as 'Theatre Against Drugs' (for addicts), 'Geetimalya' (for underprivileged children) and 'Shohaag' (for women empowerment) are well-known and have become movements.

Presently, Pranay is collating his discourses on mind-body-spirit themes for various book series.

Connect with him on his website: pranay.org